Irish Swear Word Coloring Book

By: Shazza T. Jones

Introduction

Learn some Irish swear words while you sit back and colour the pages.

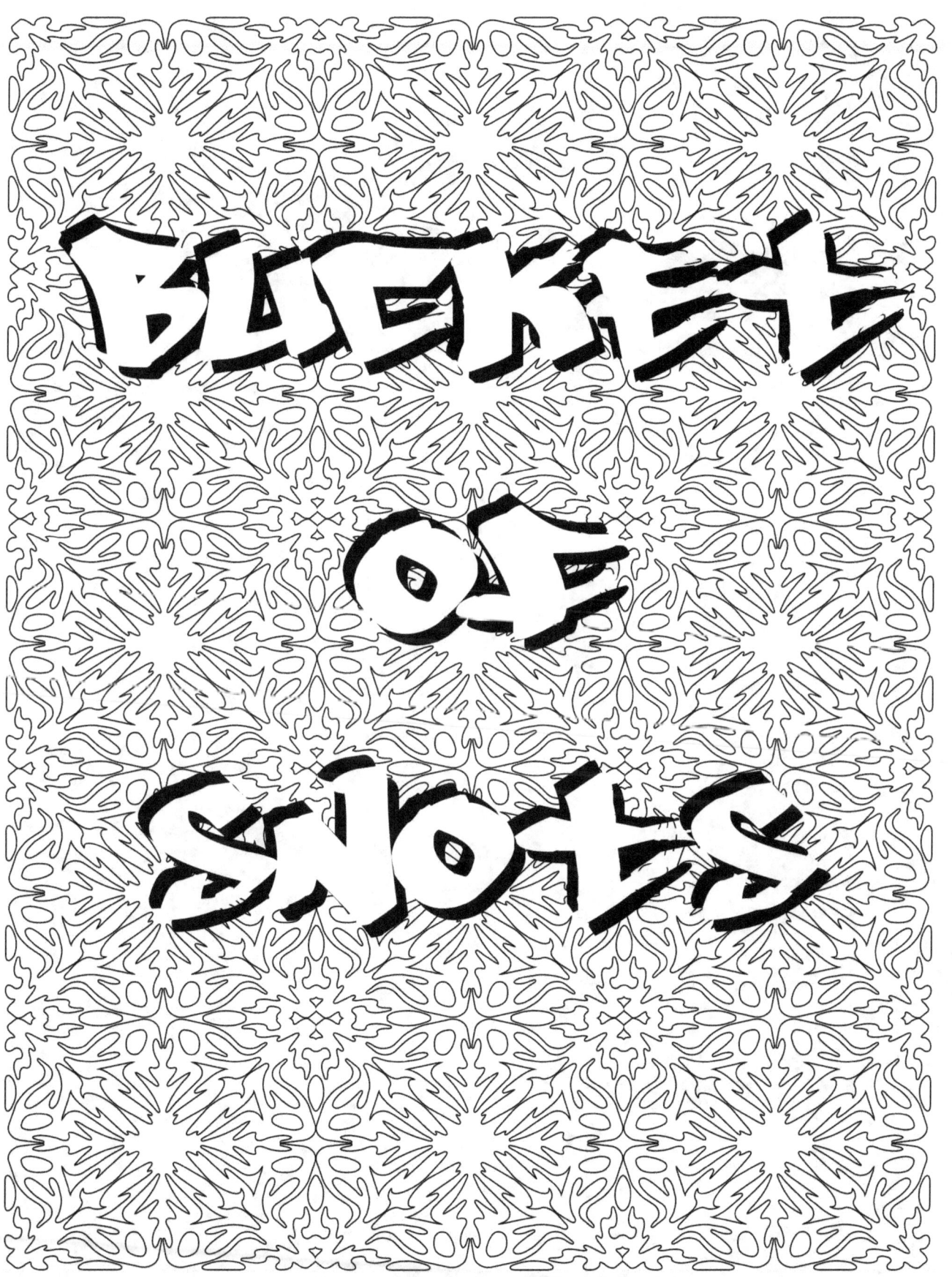

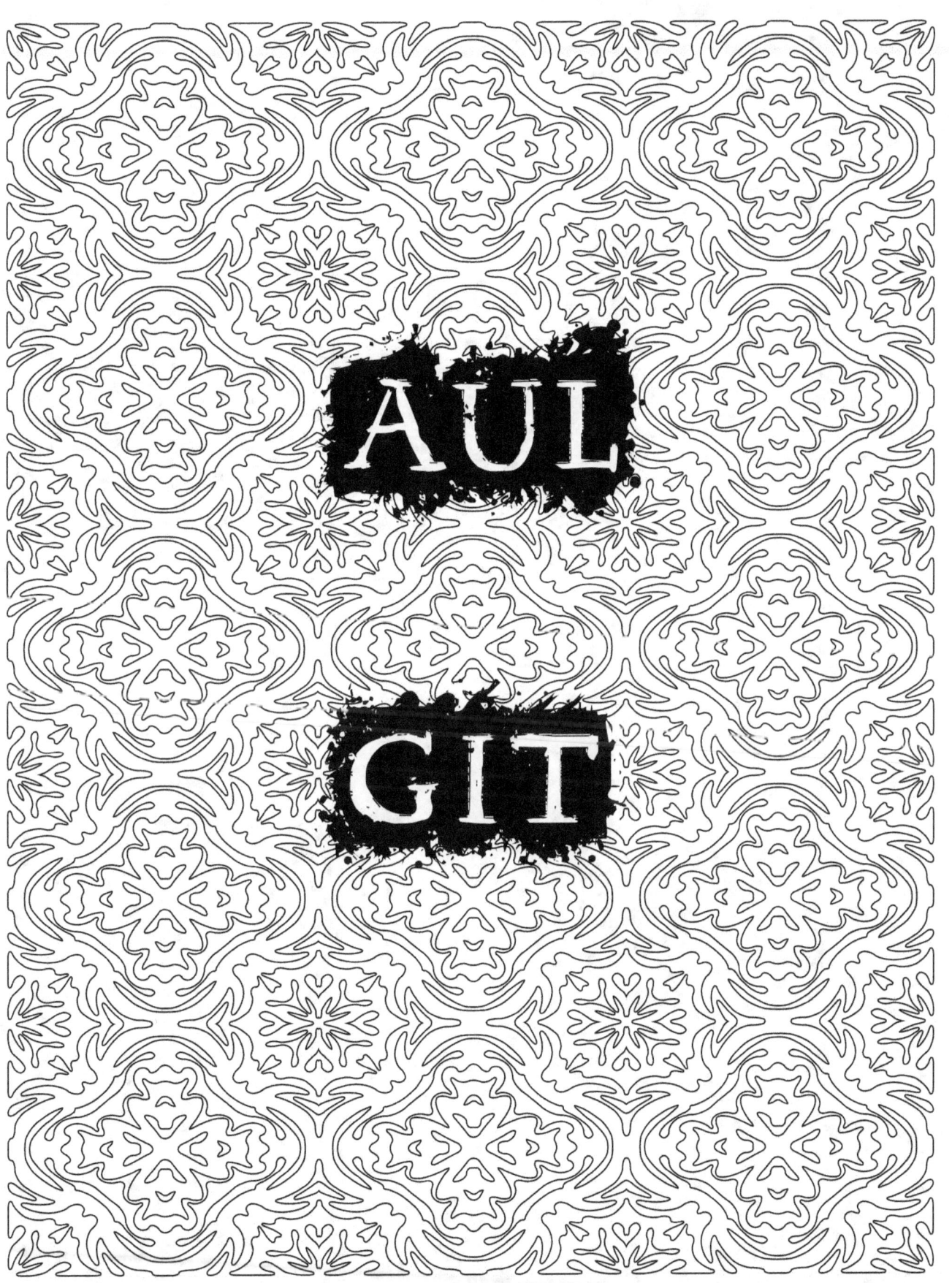

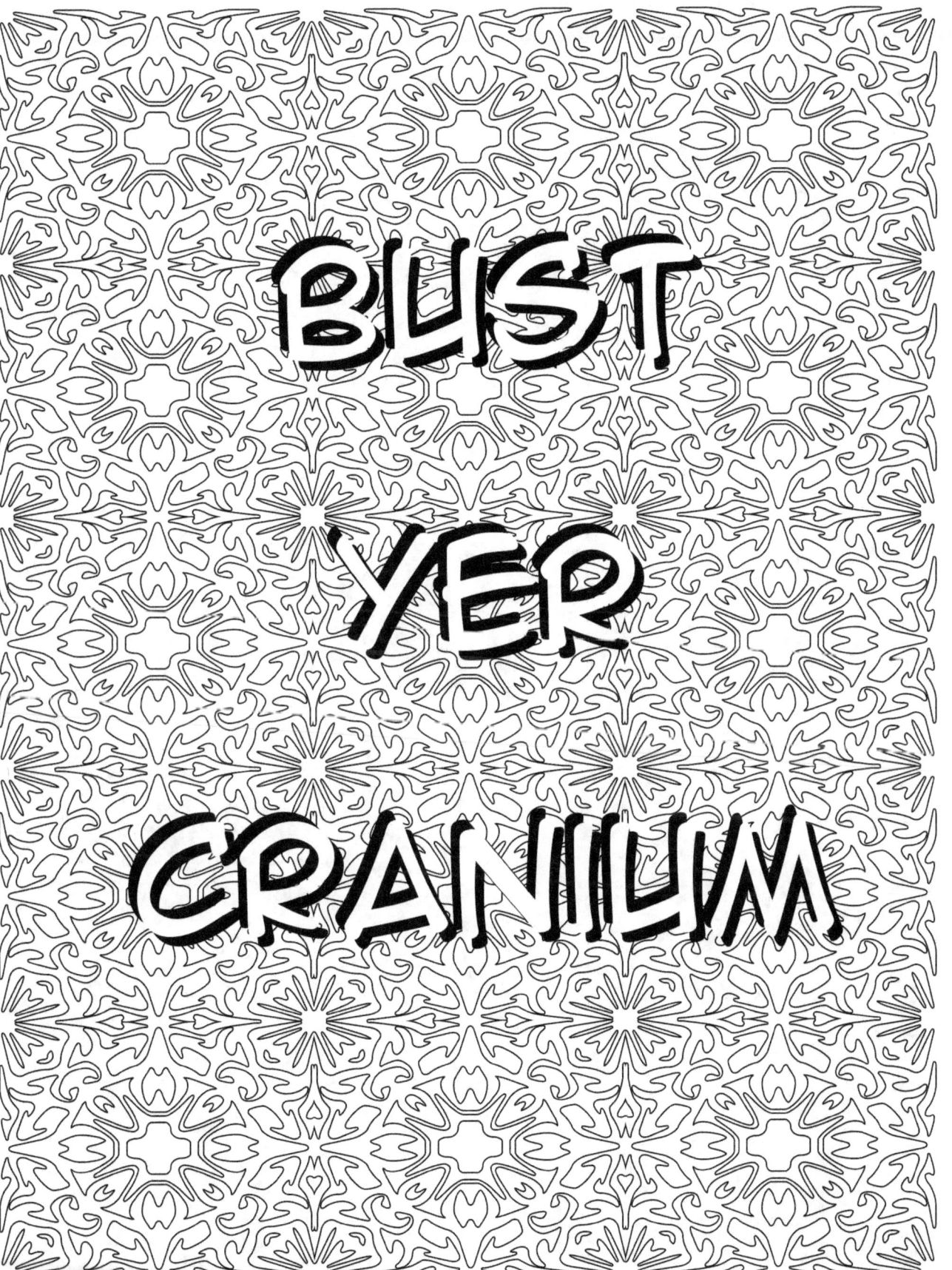

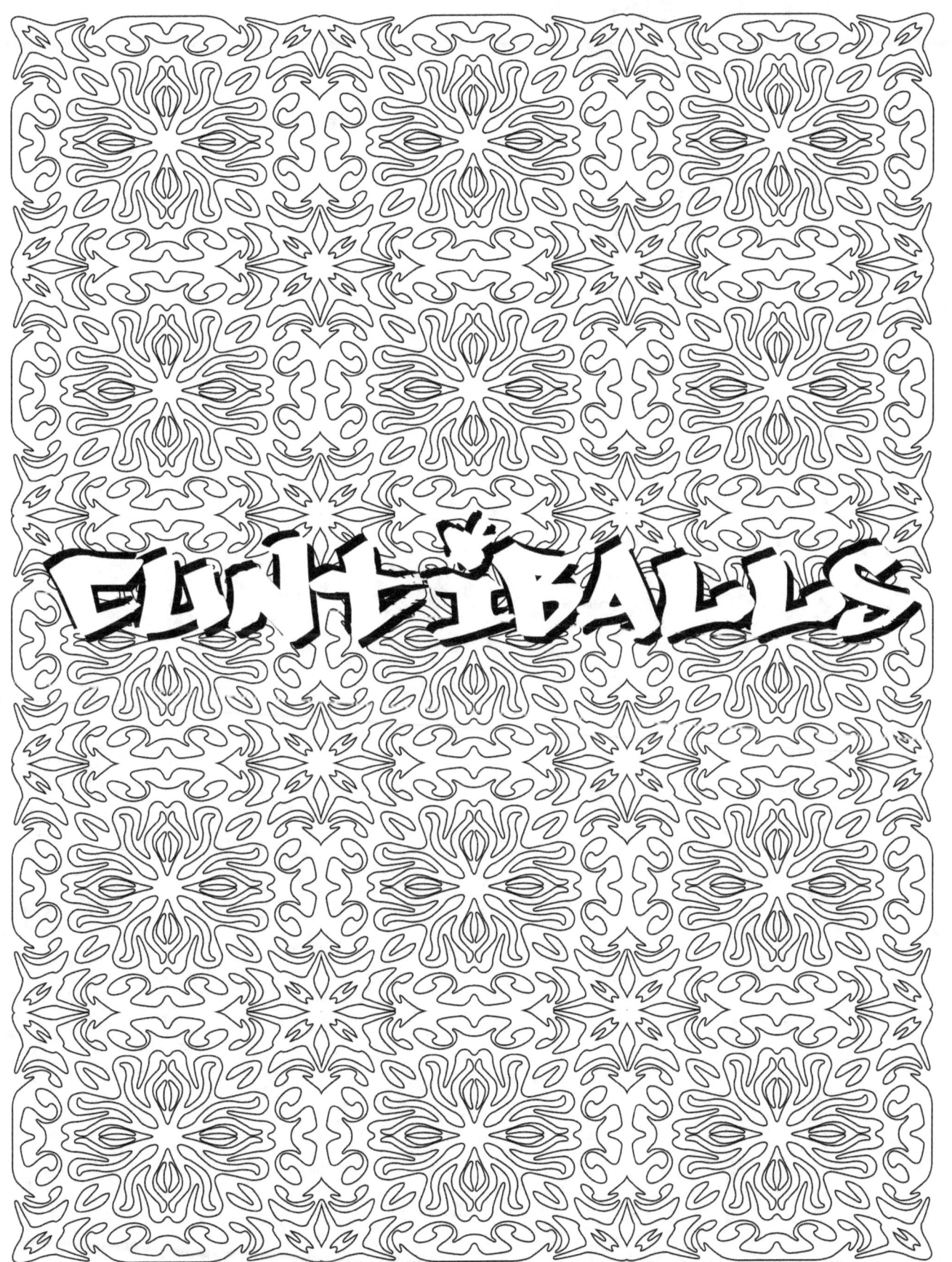

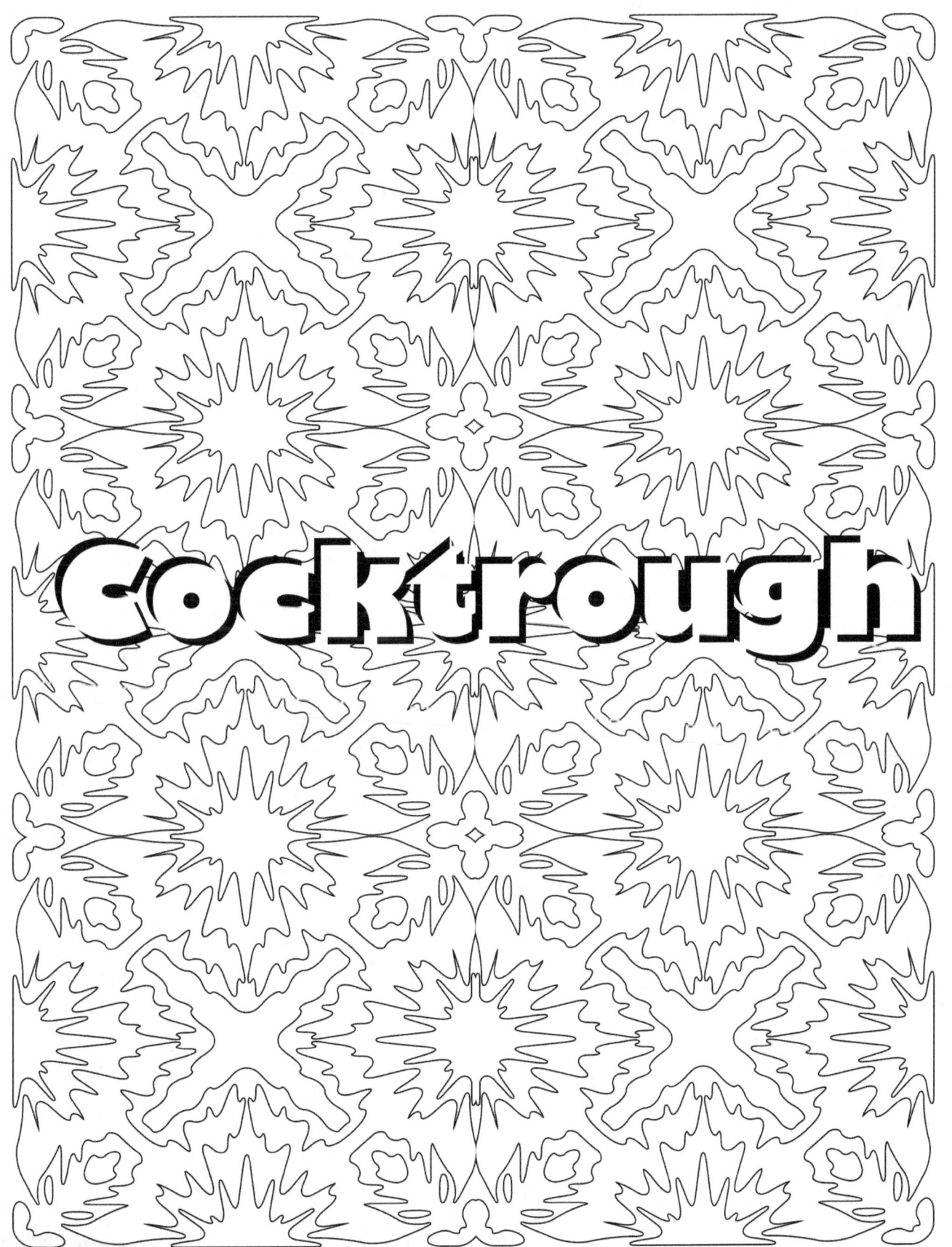

Cocktrough

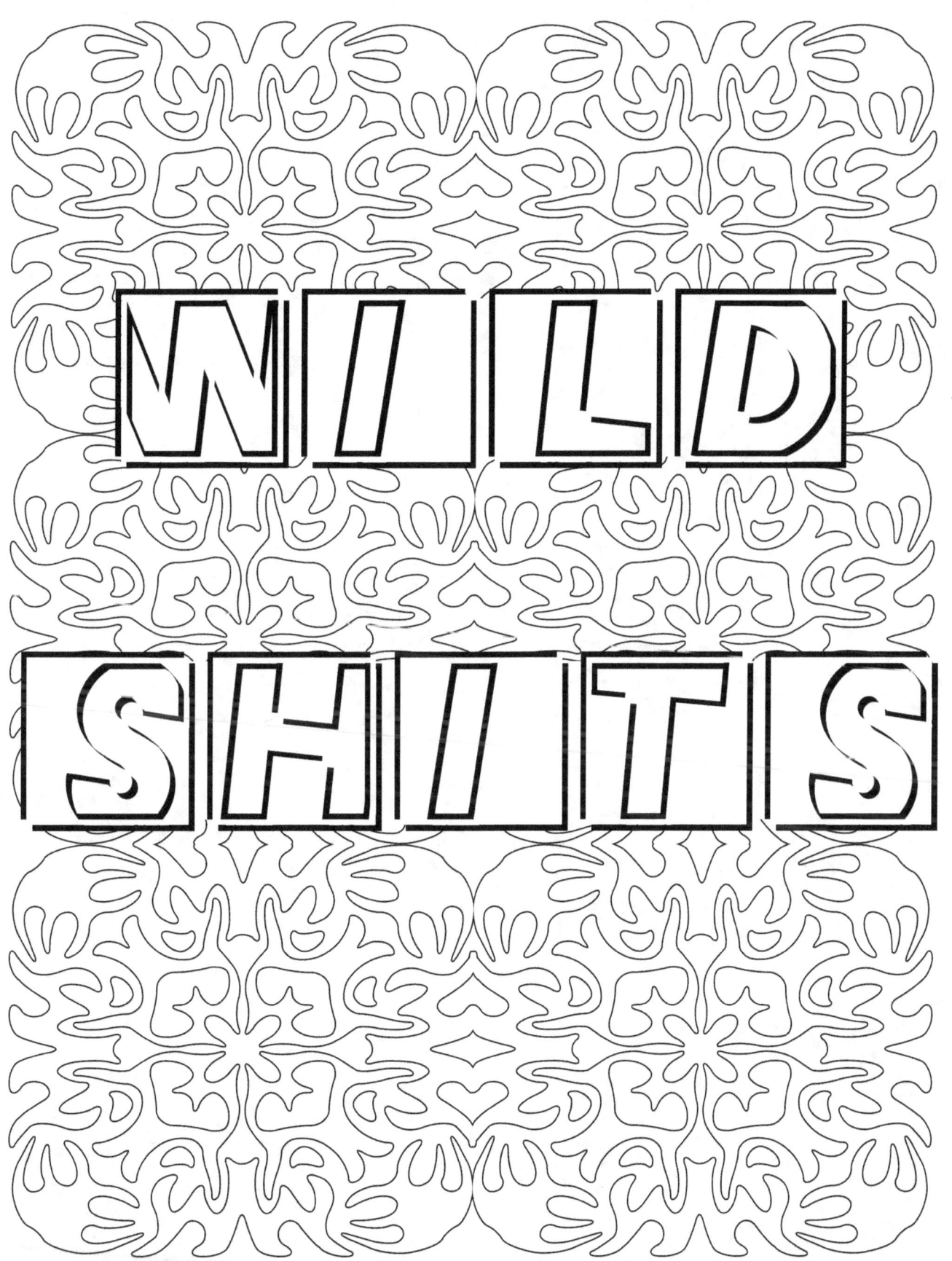

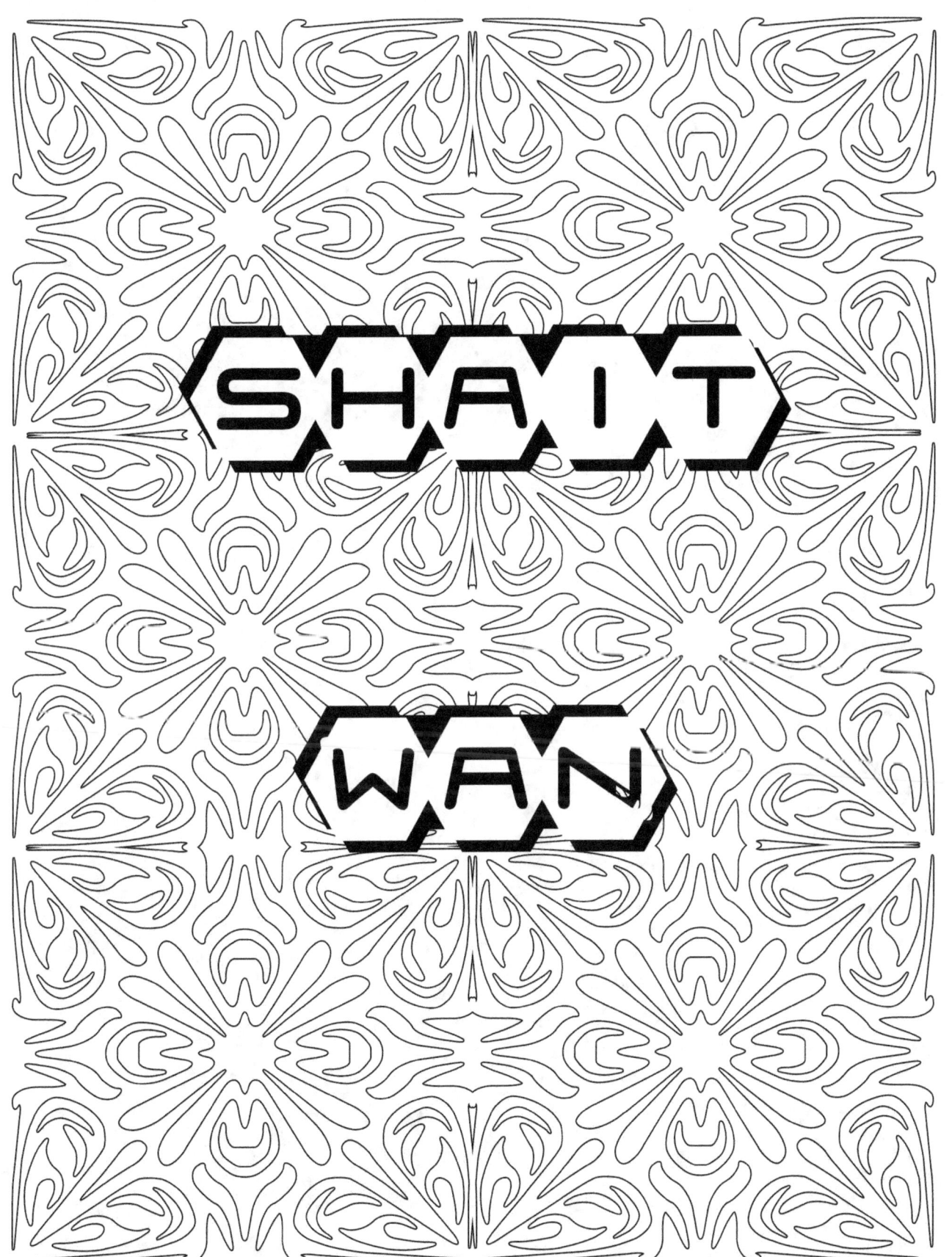

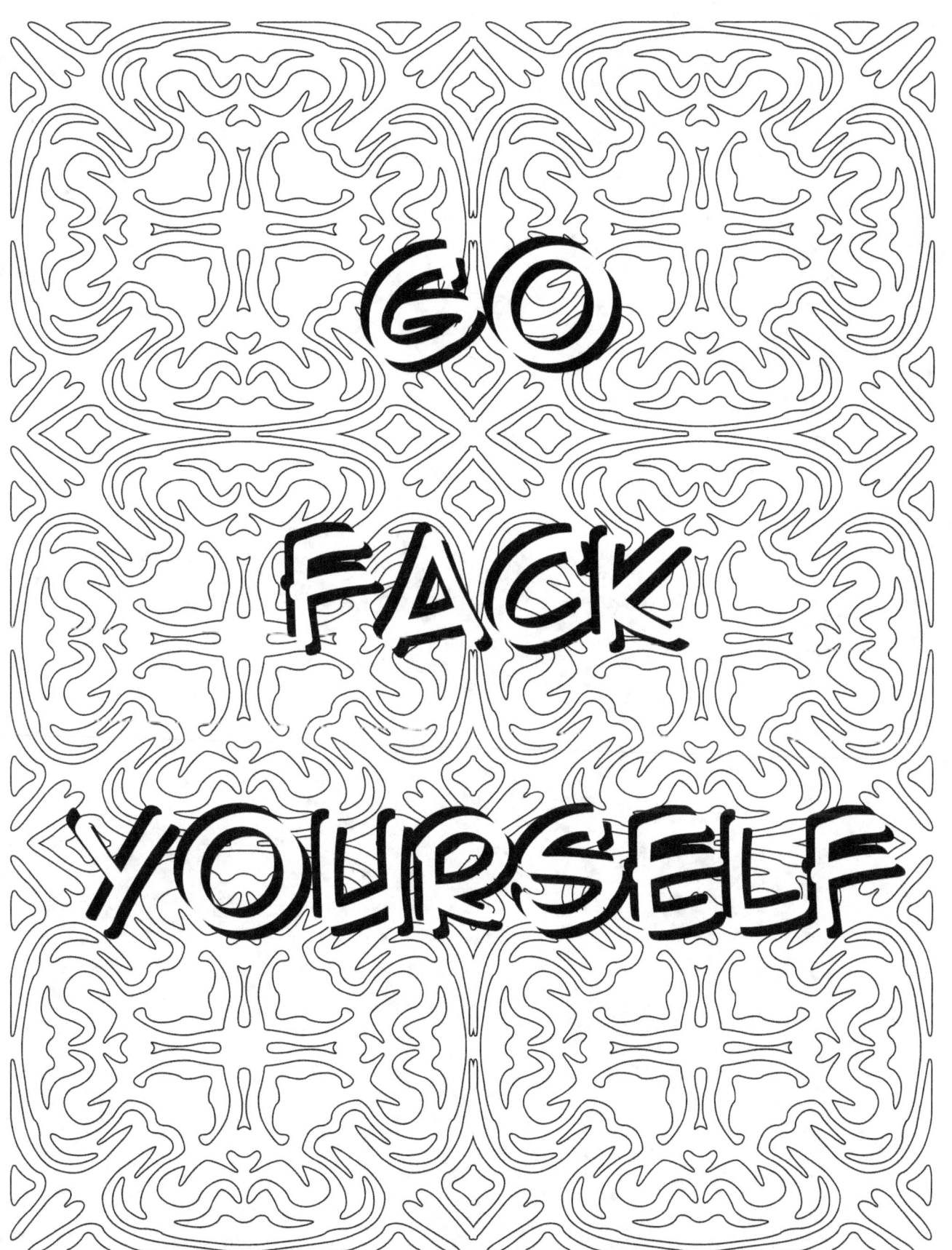

Empty the bag

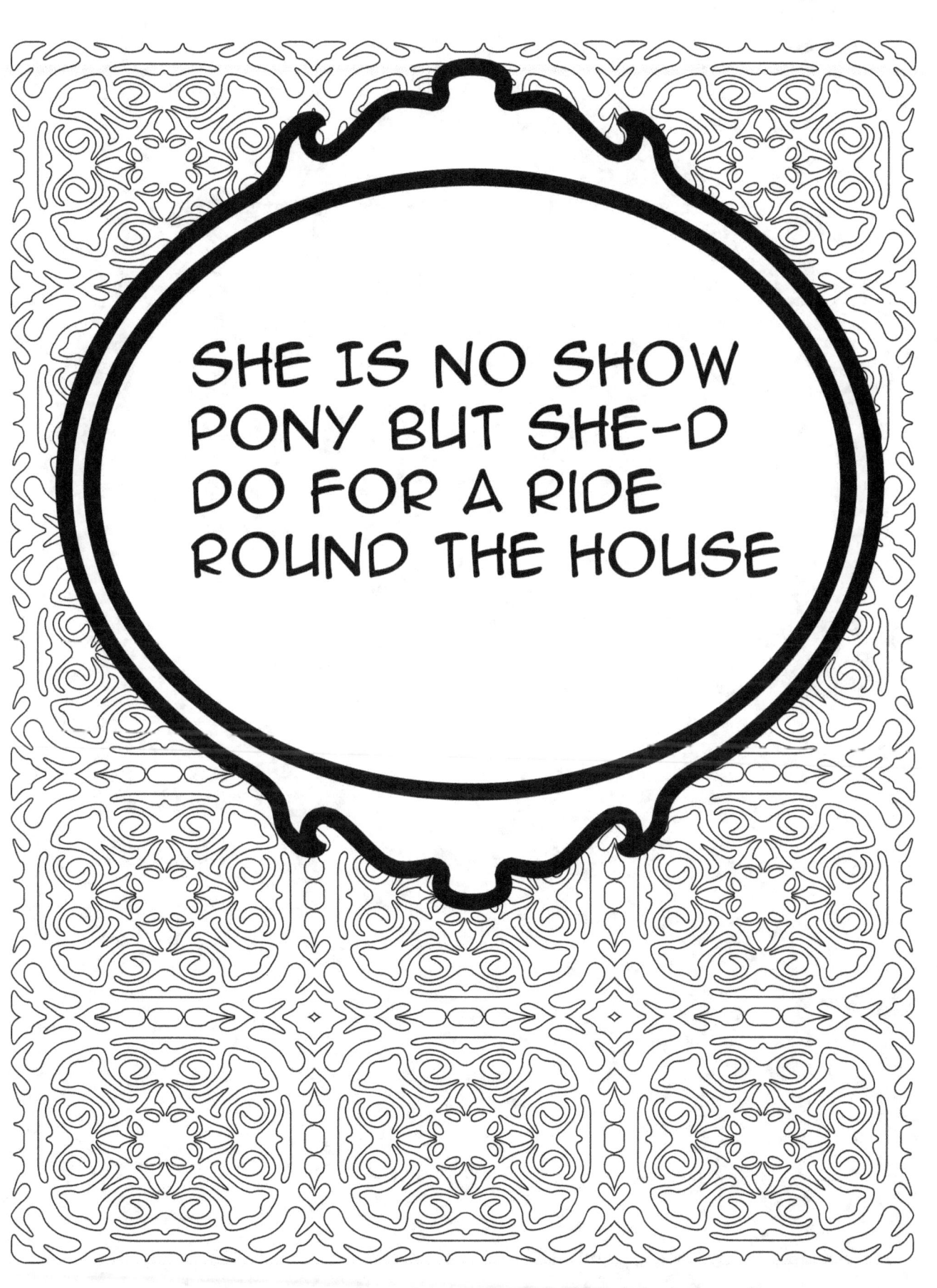

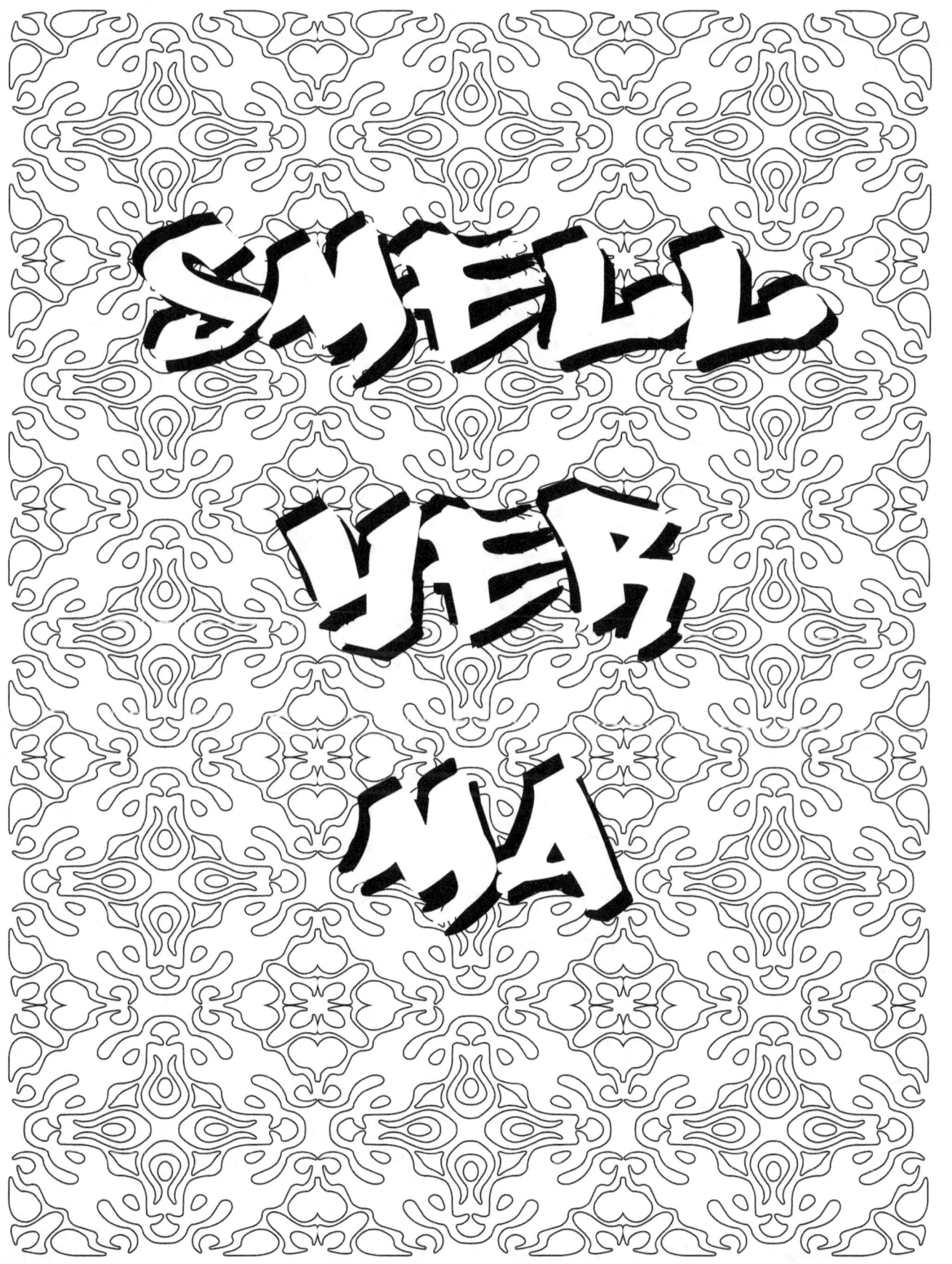

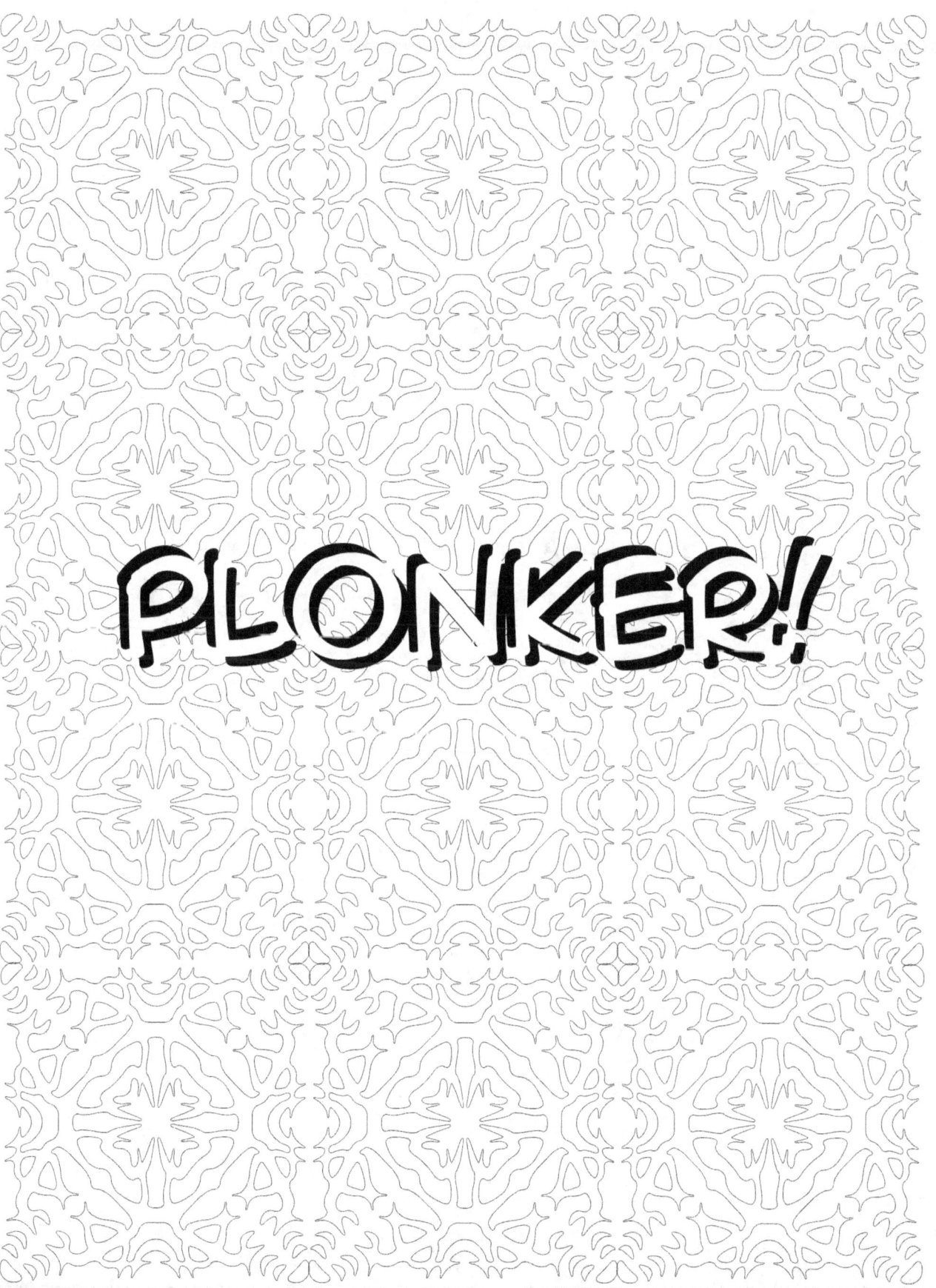

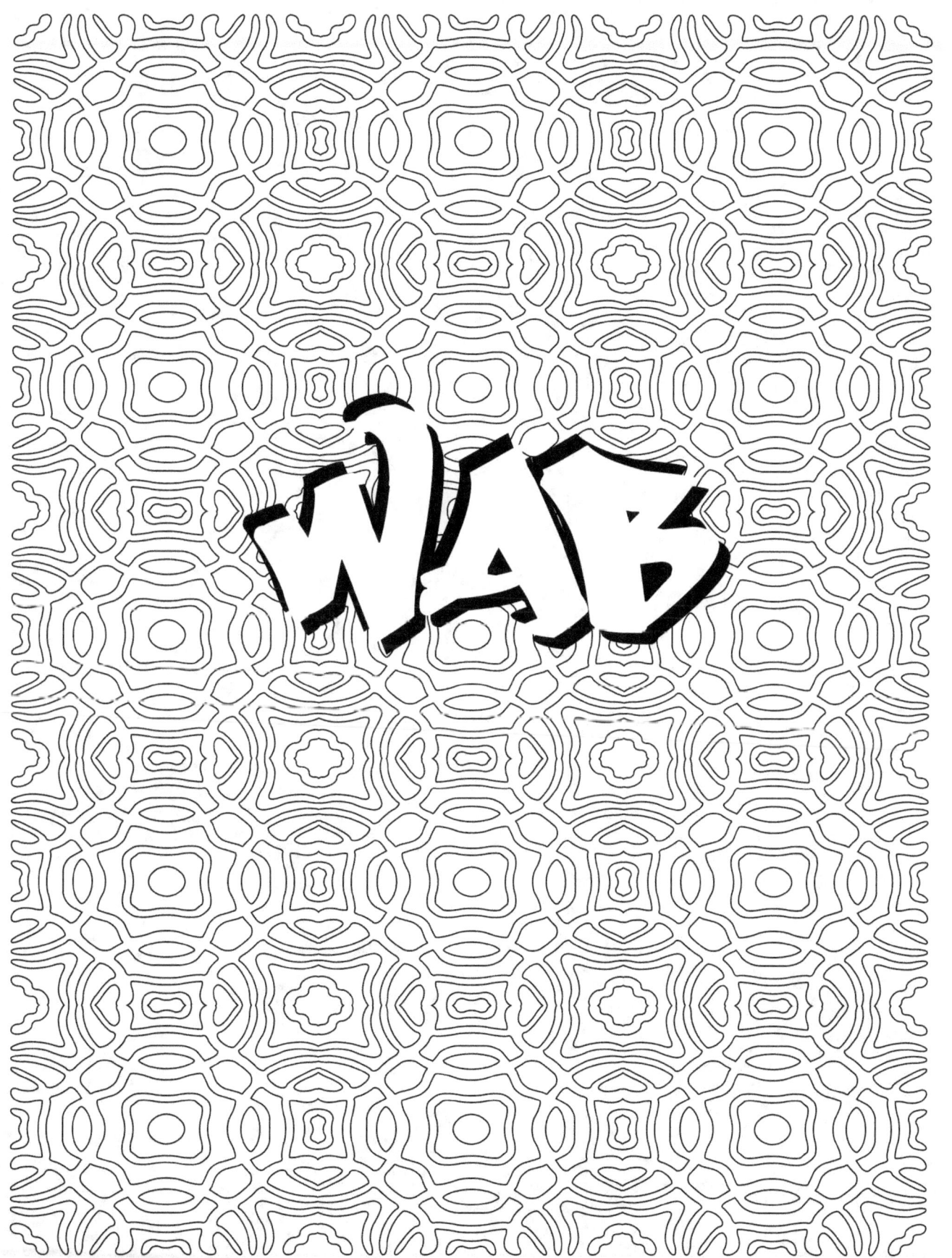

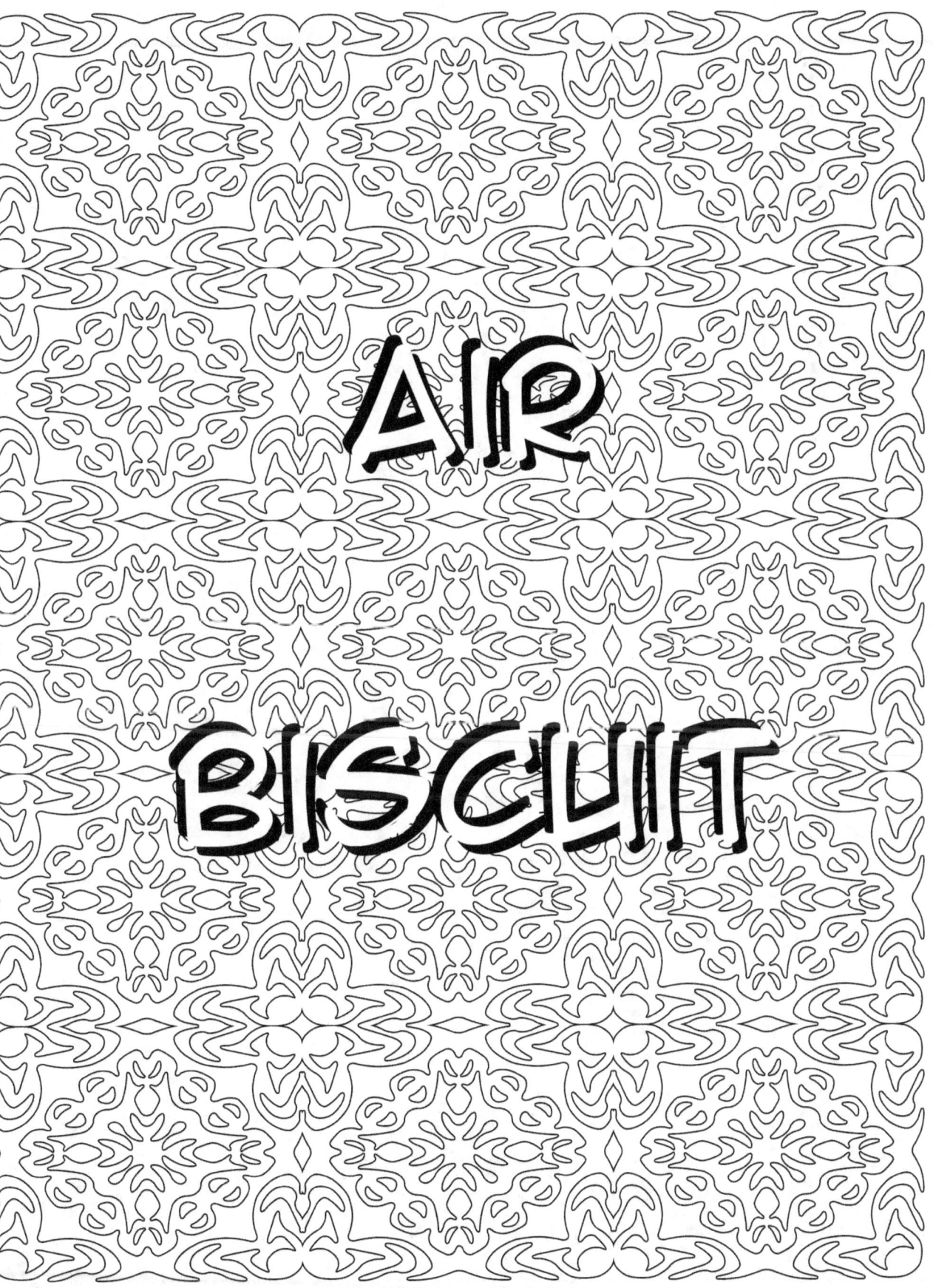

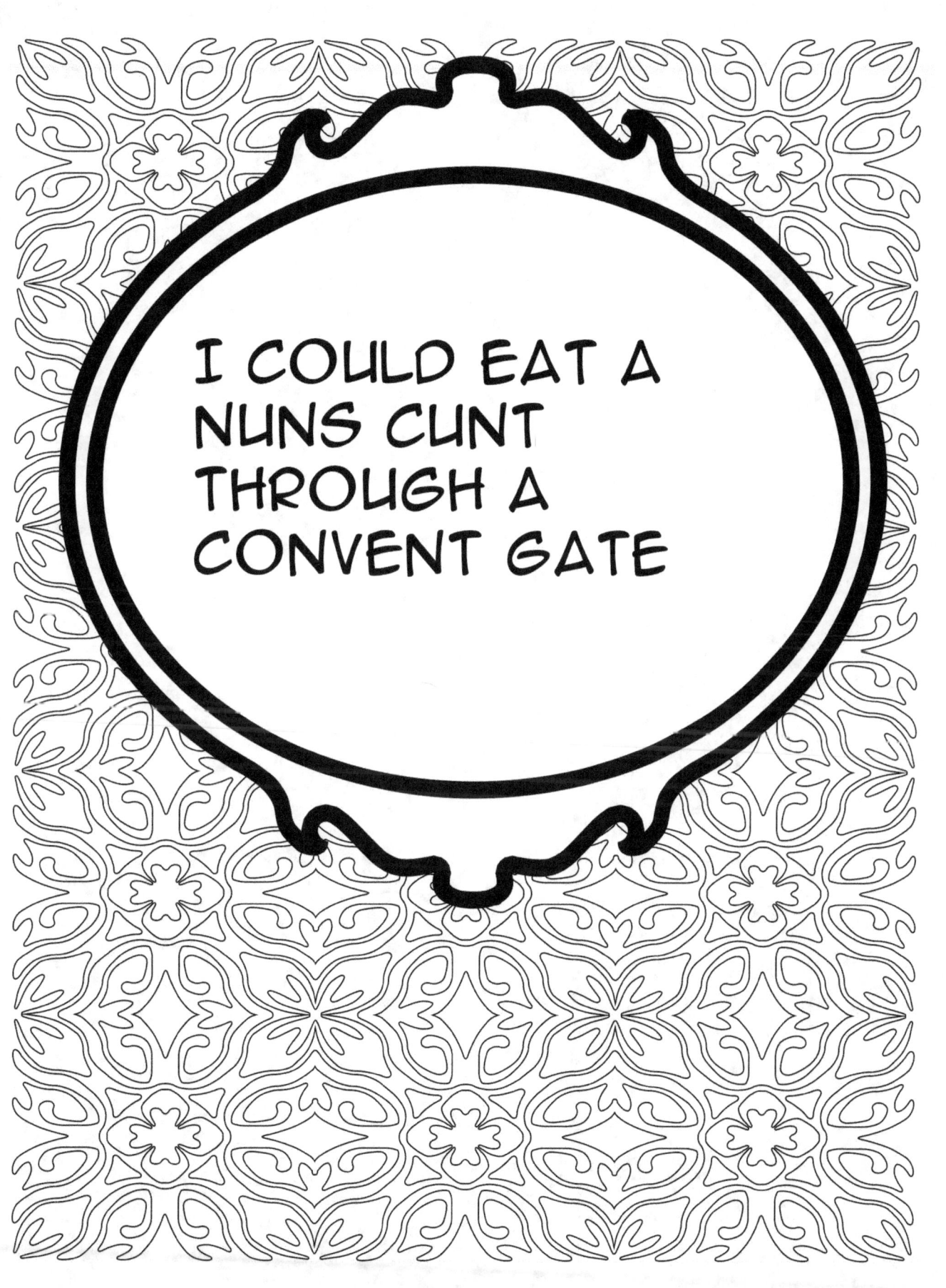

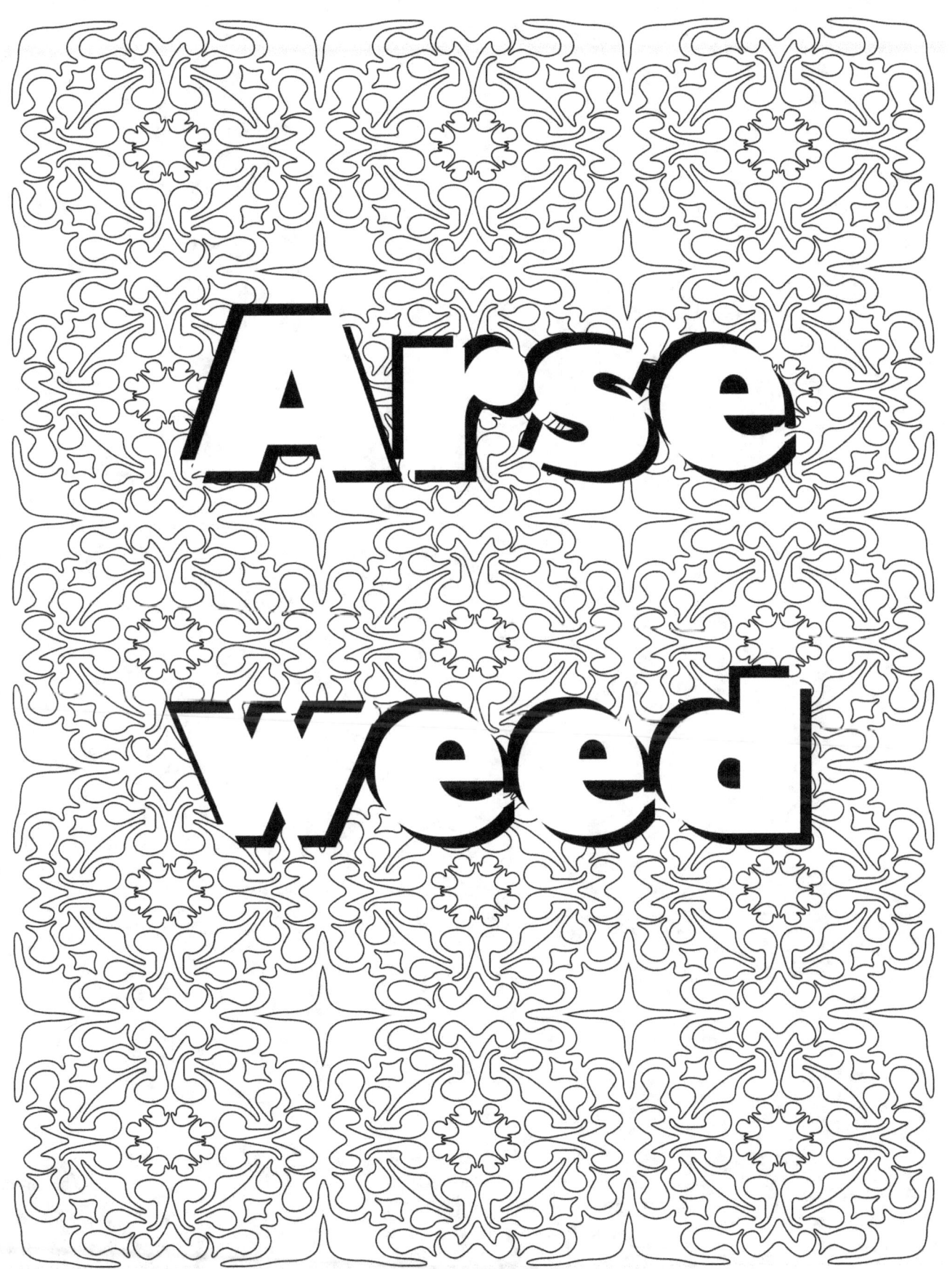

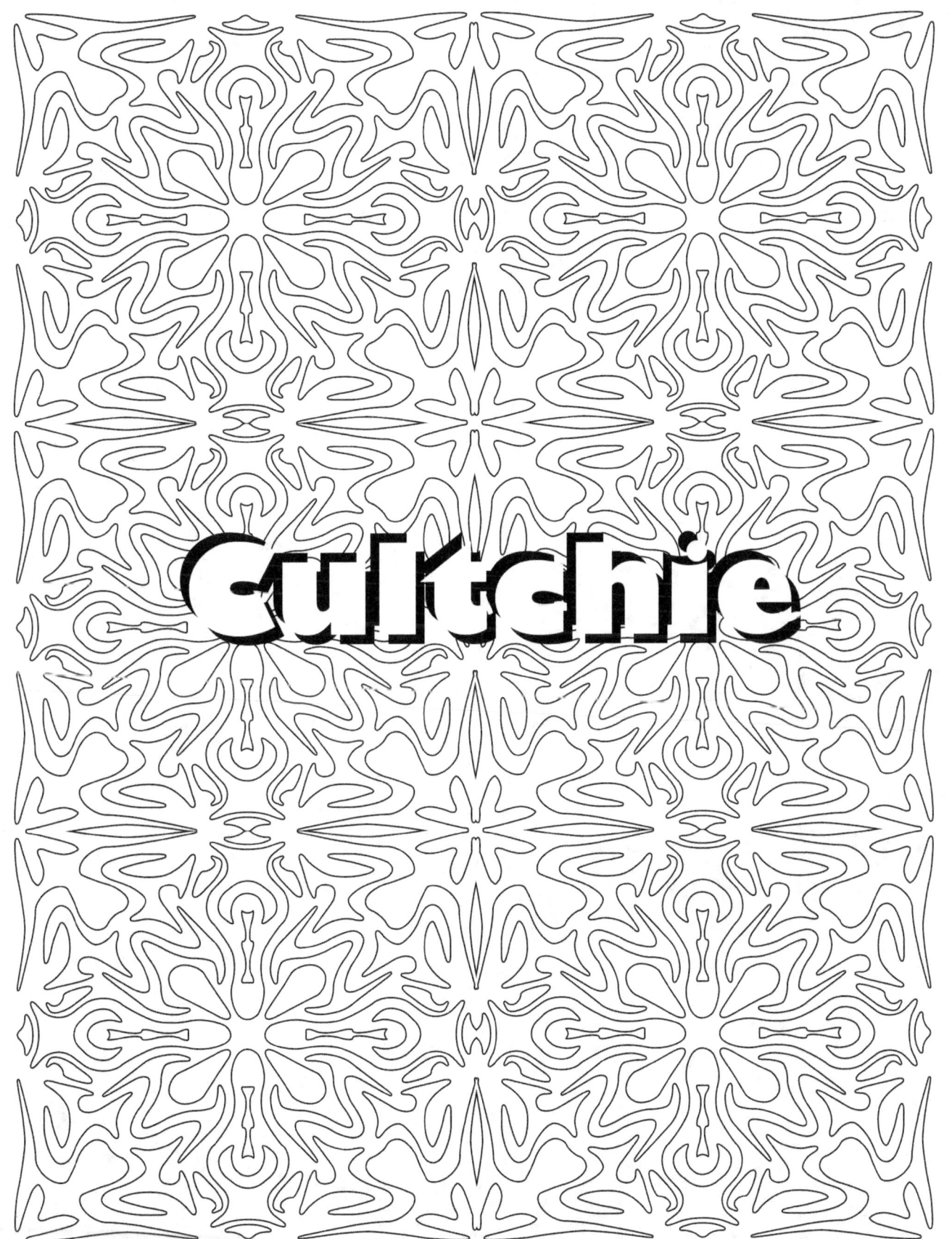

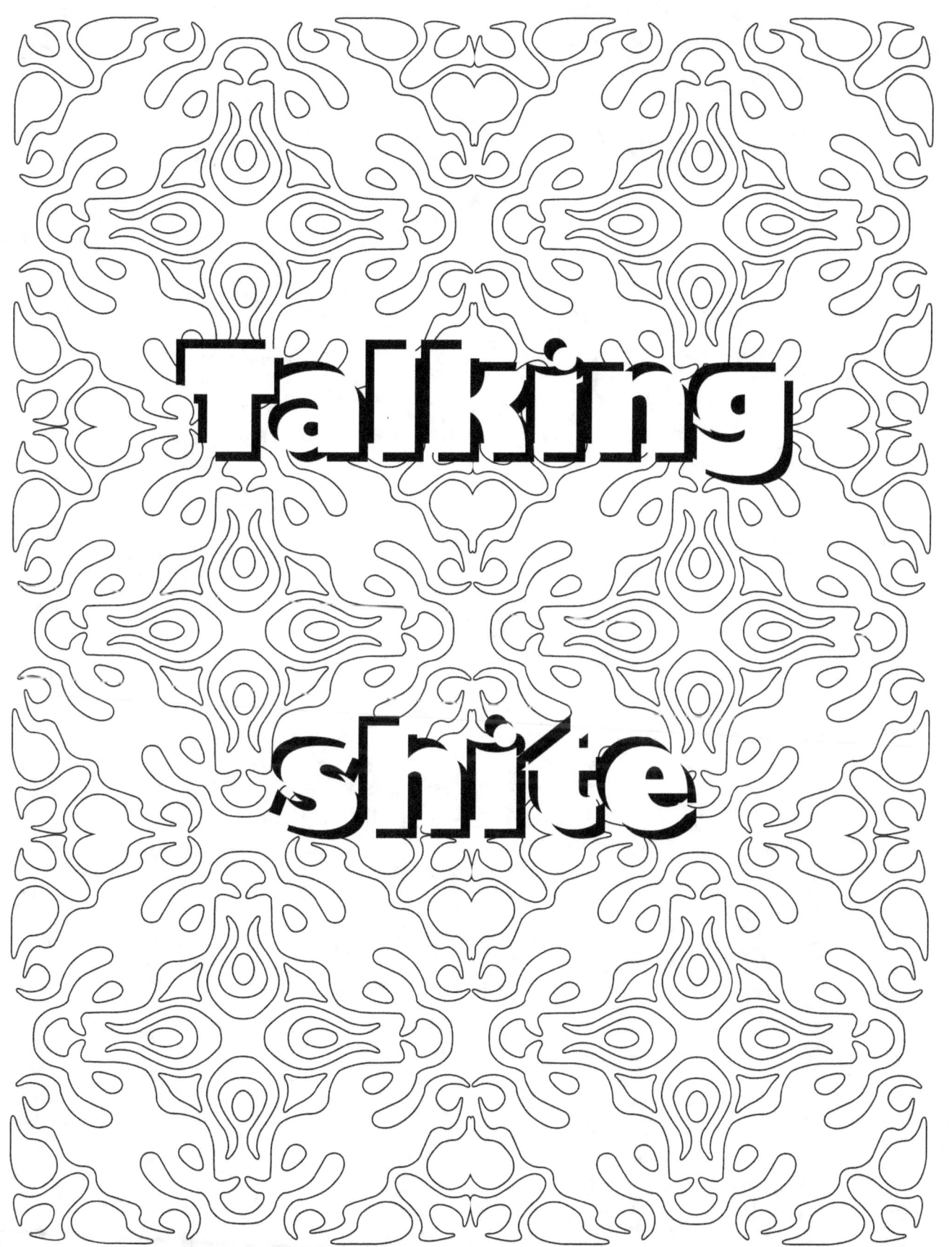

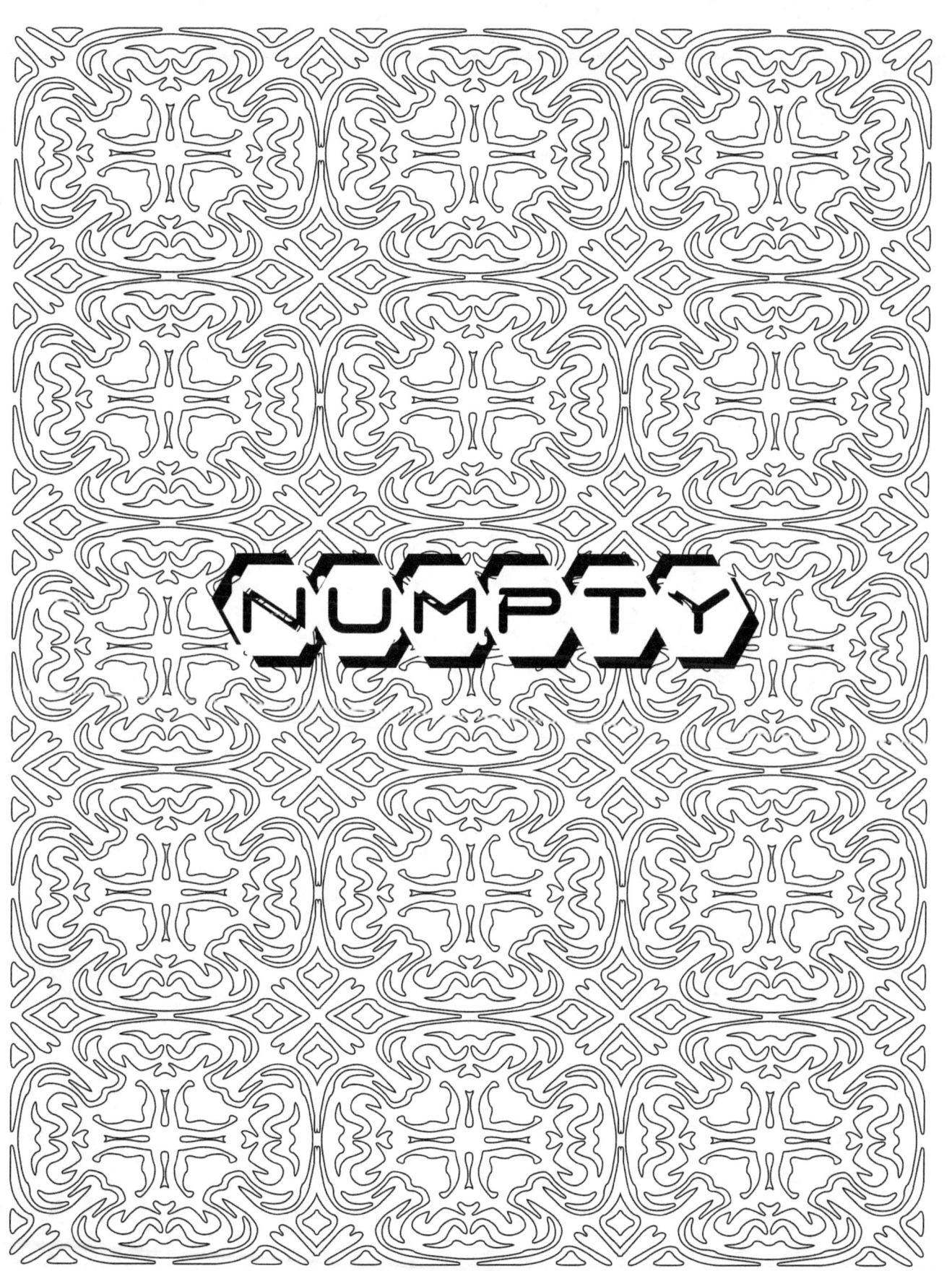

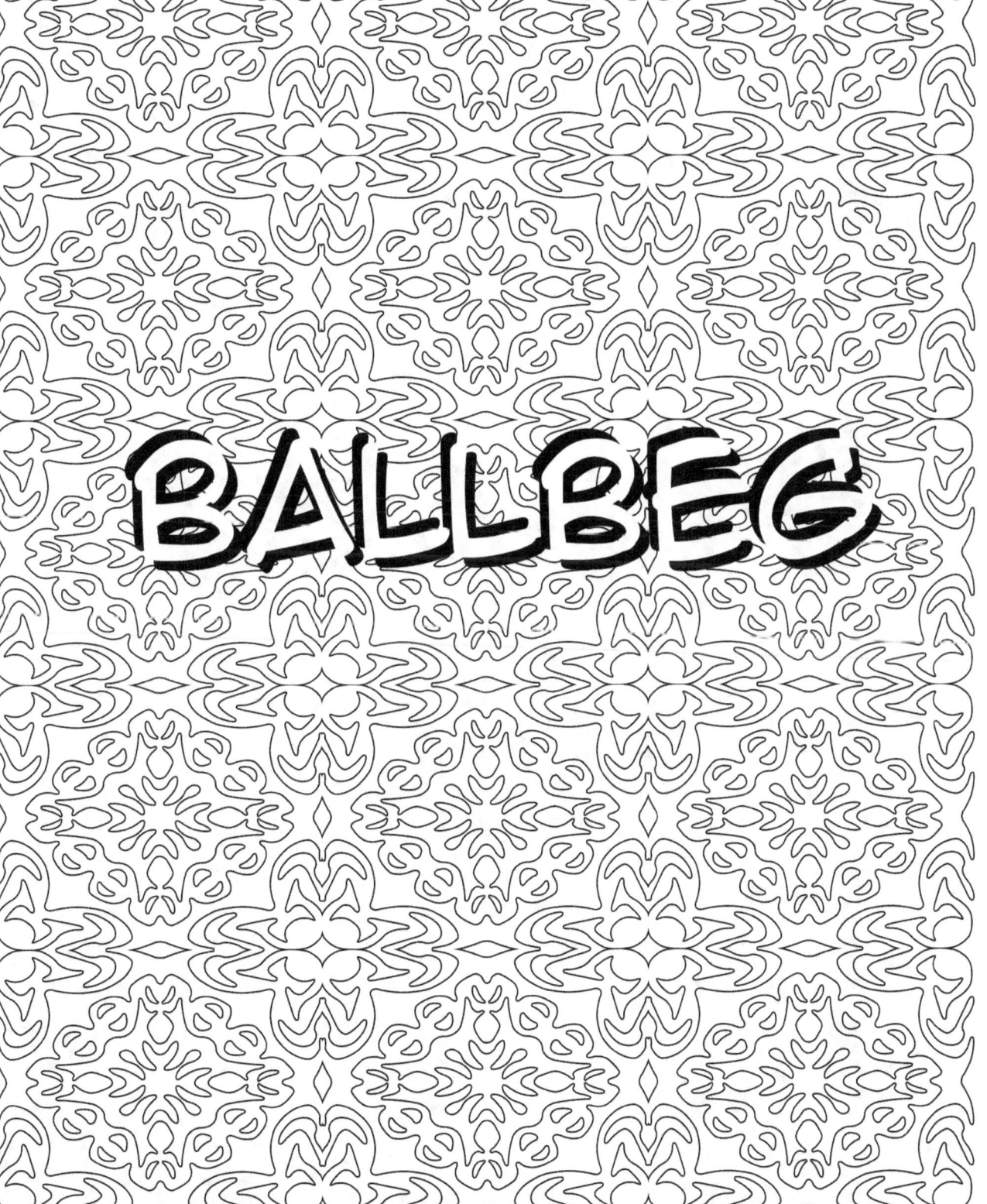

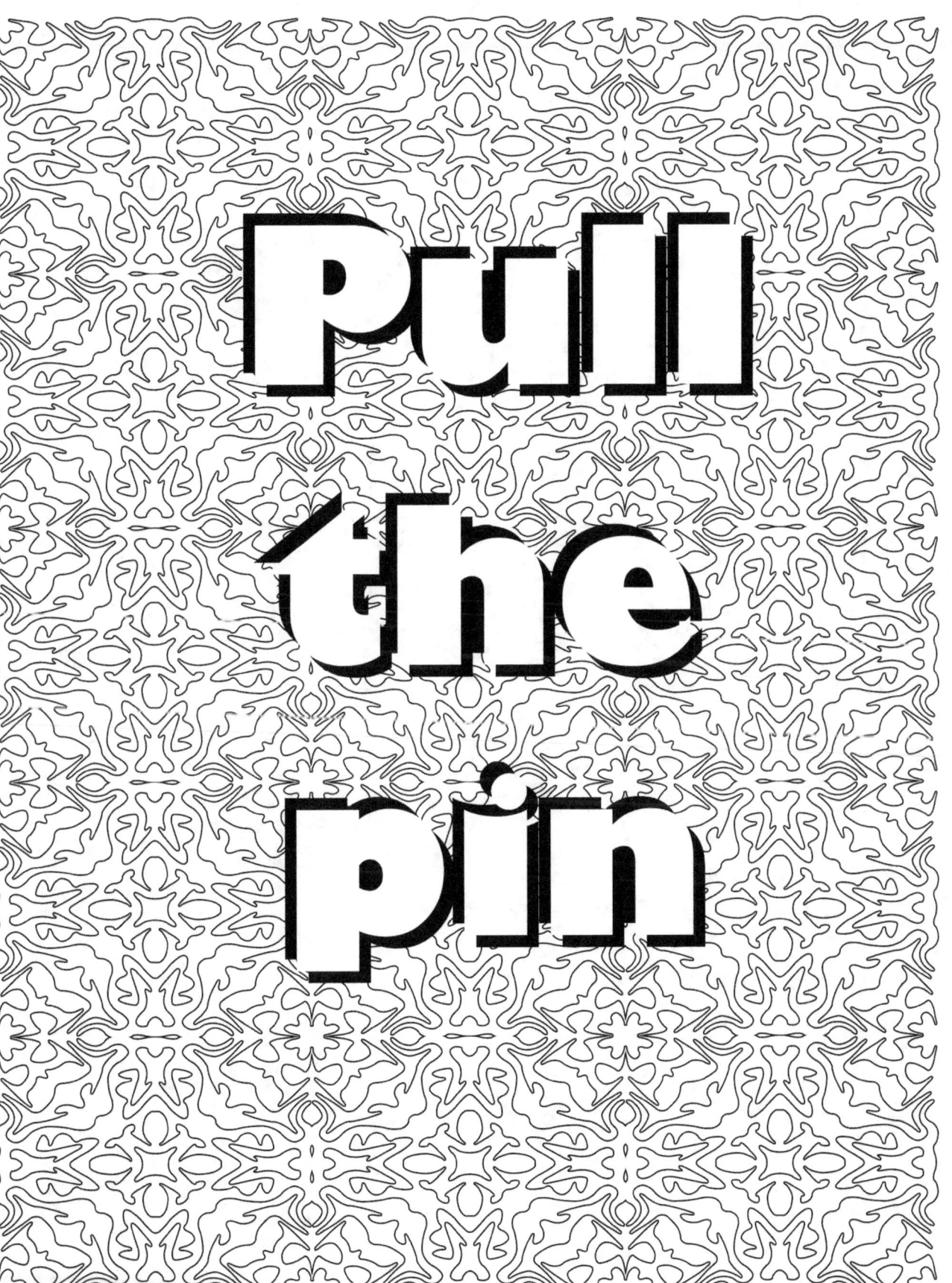

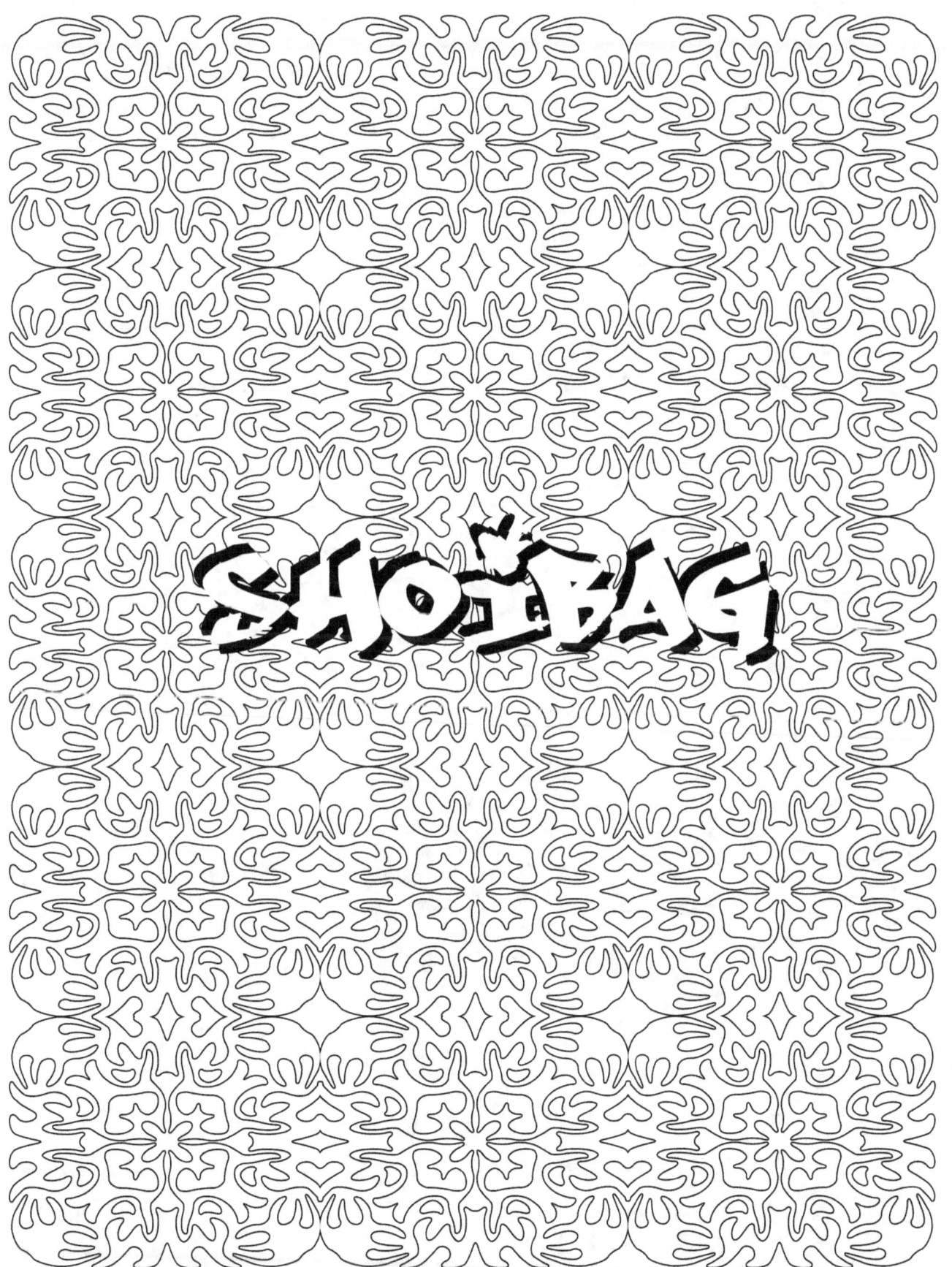

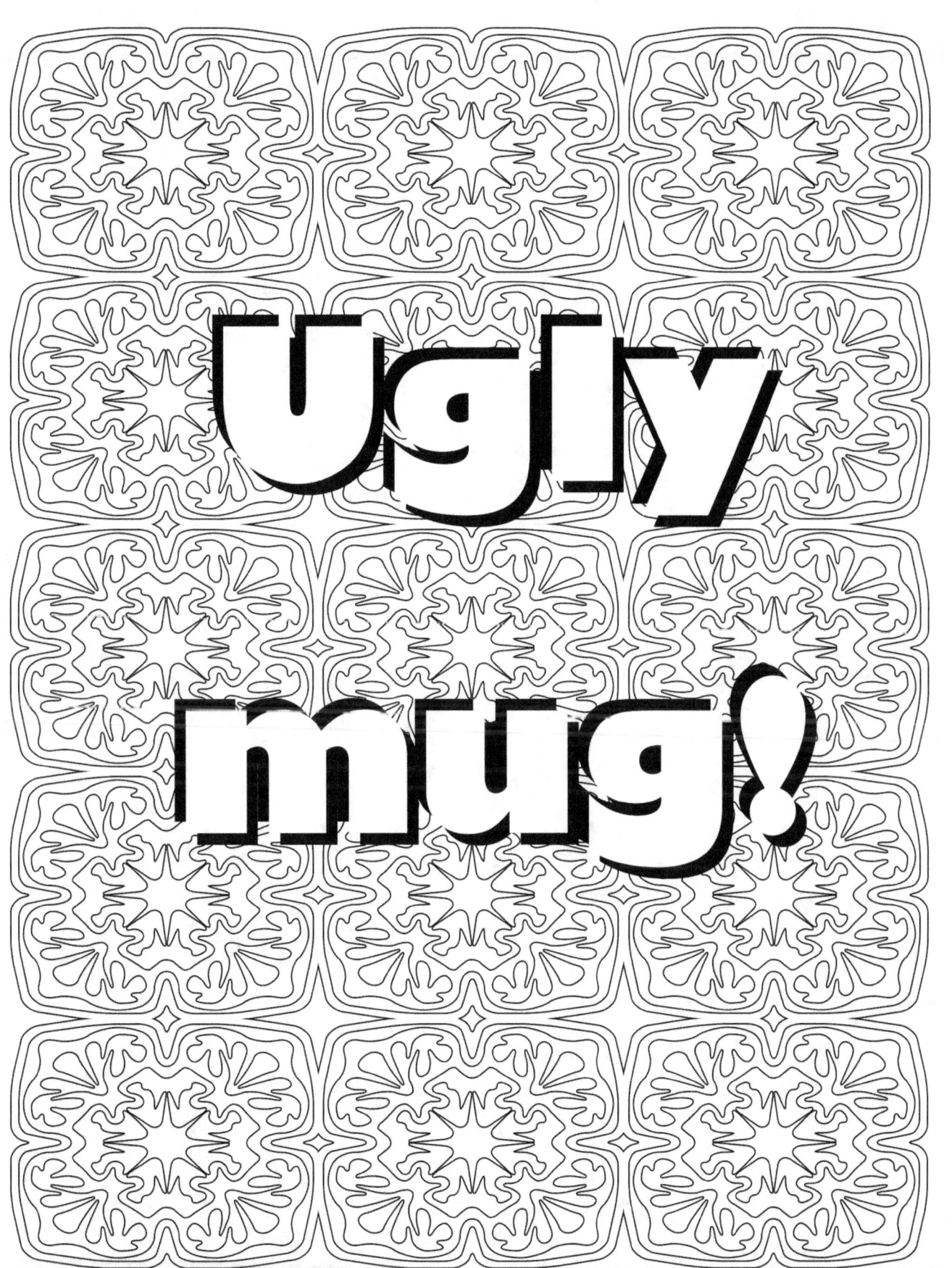

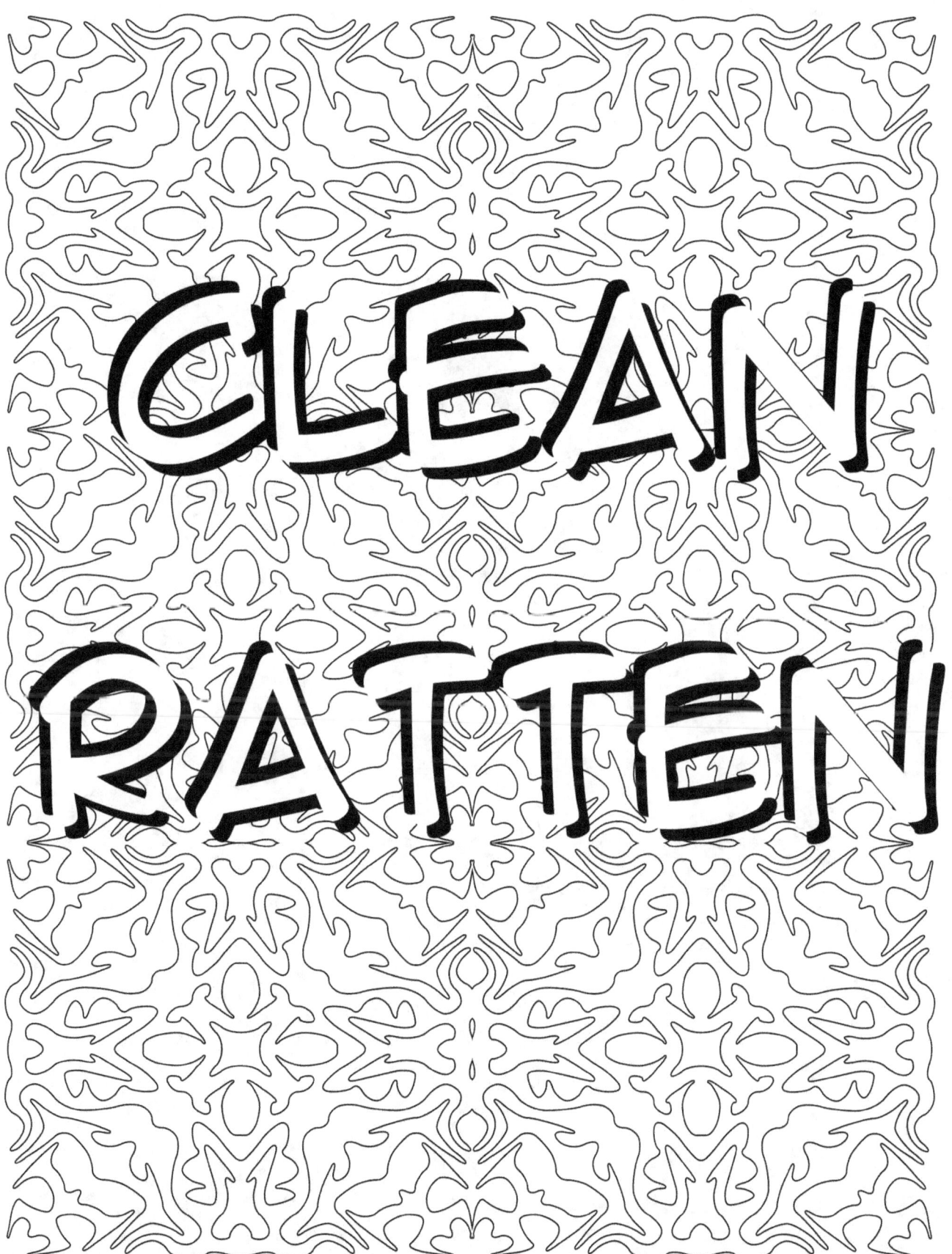

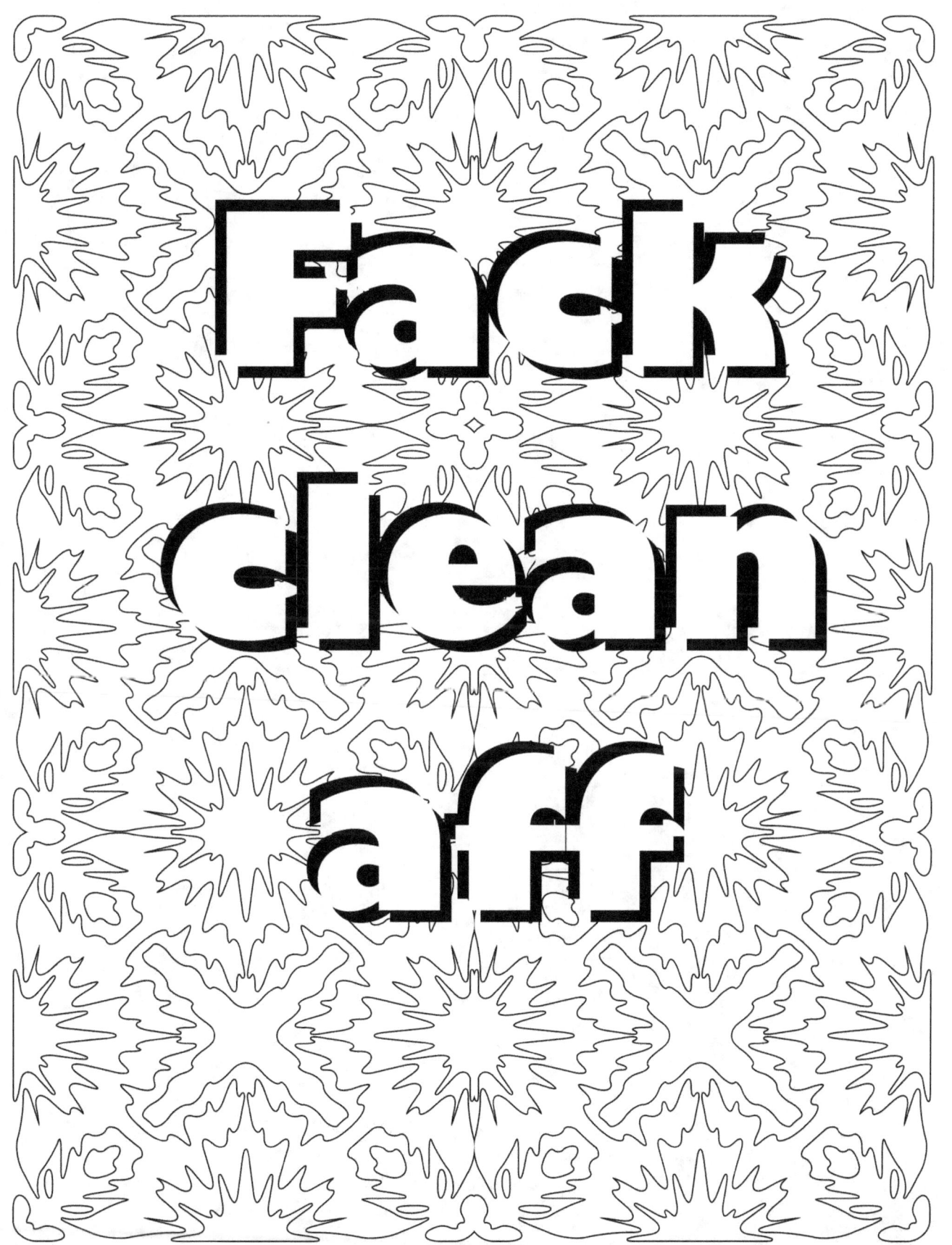

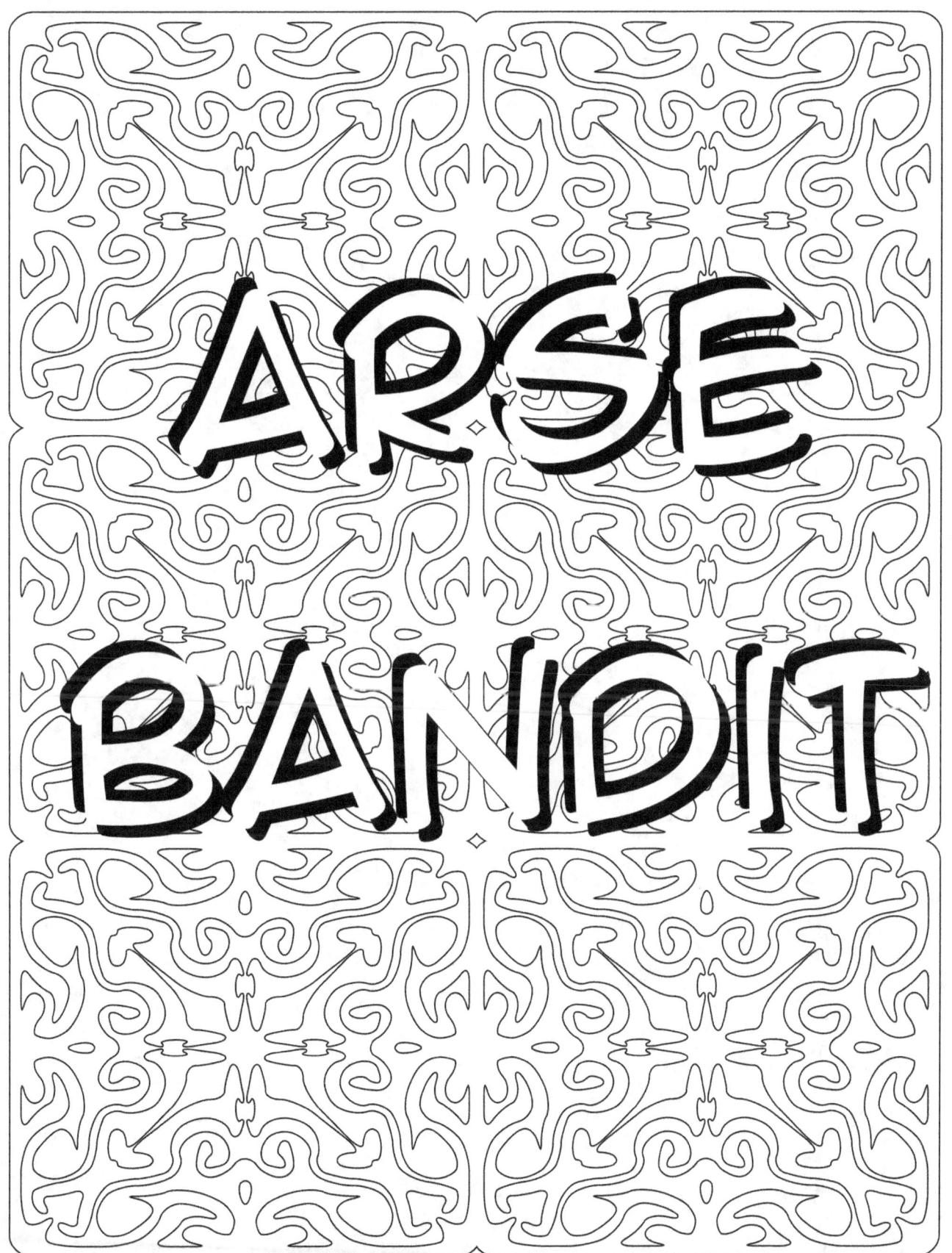

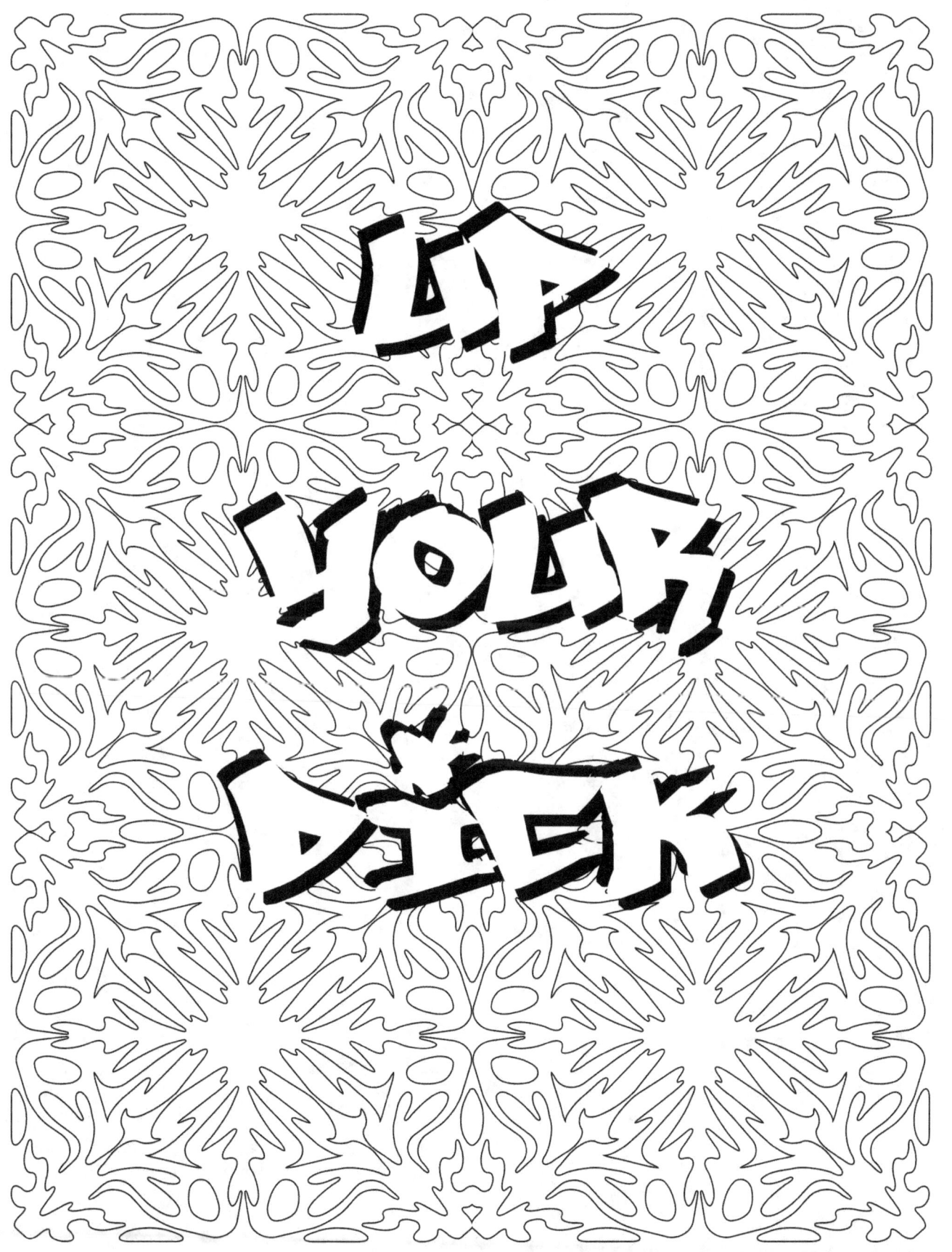

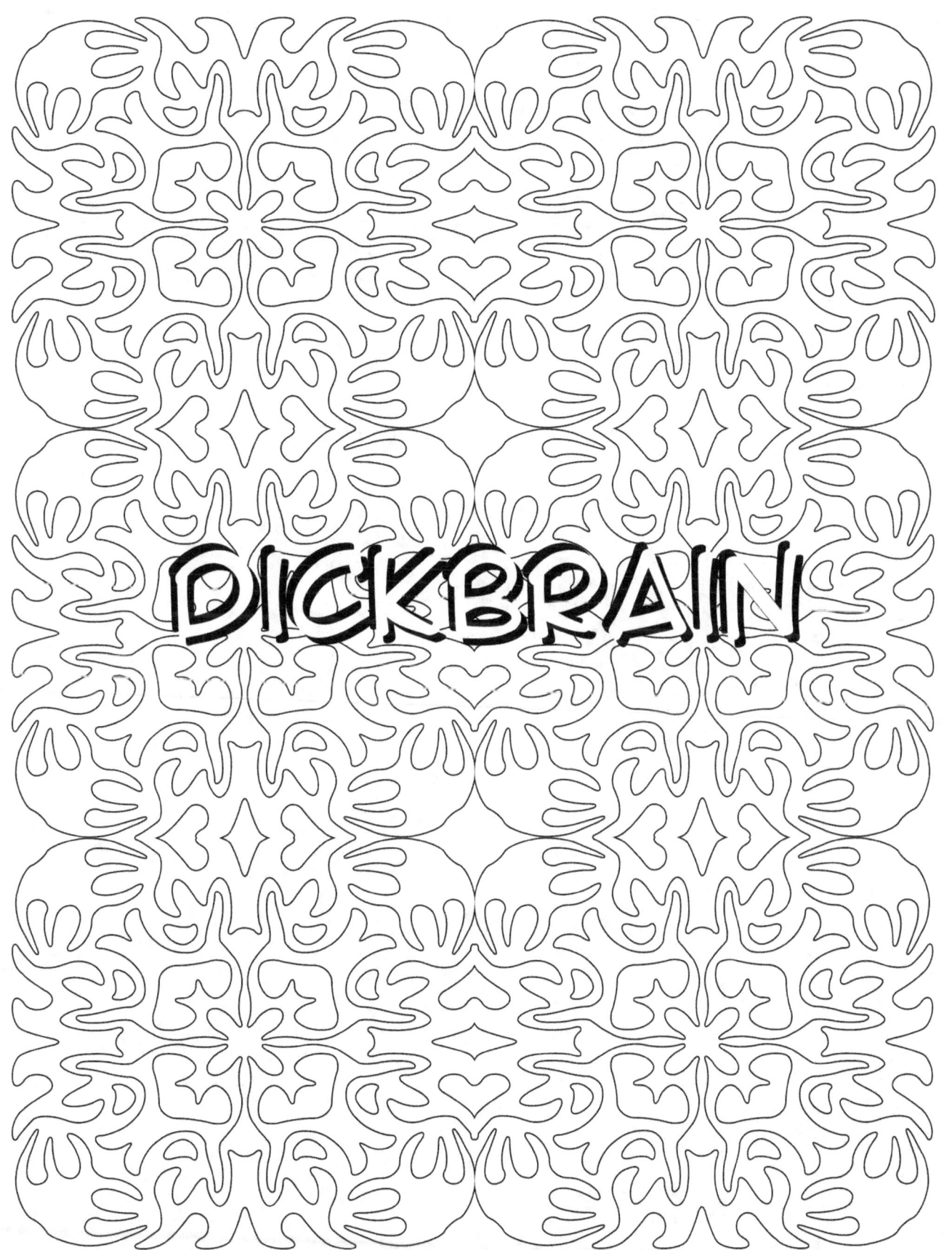

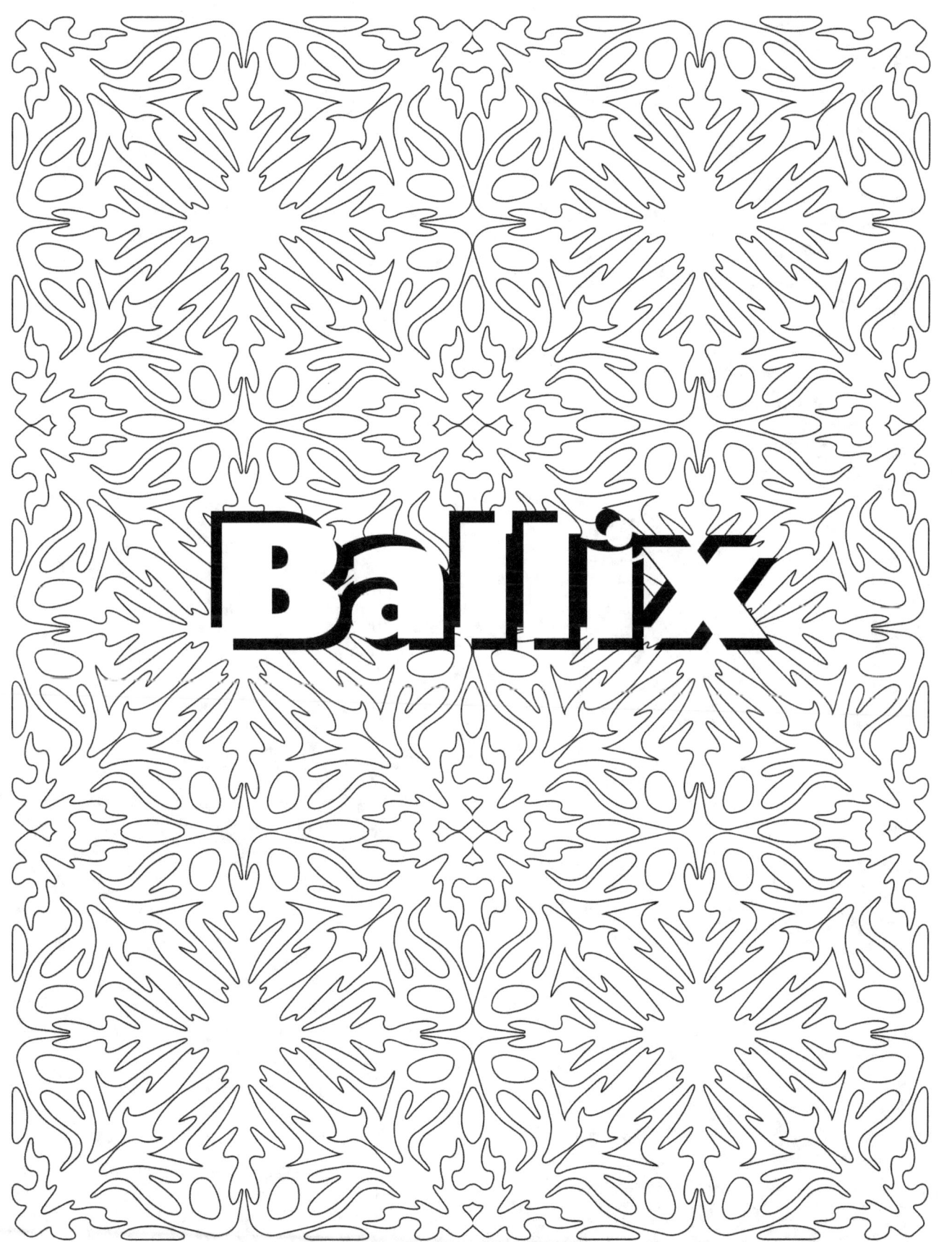

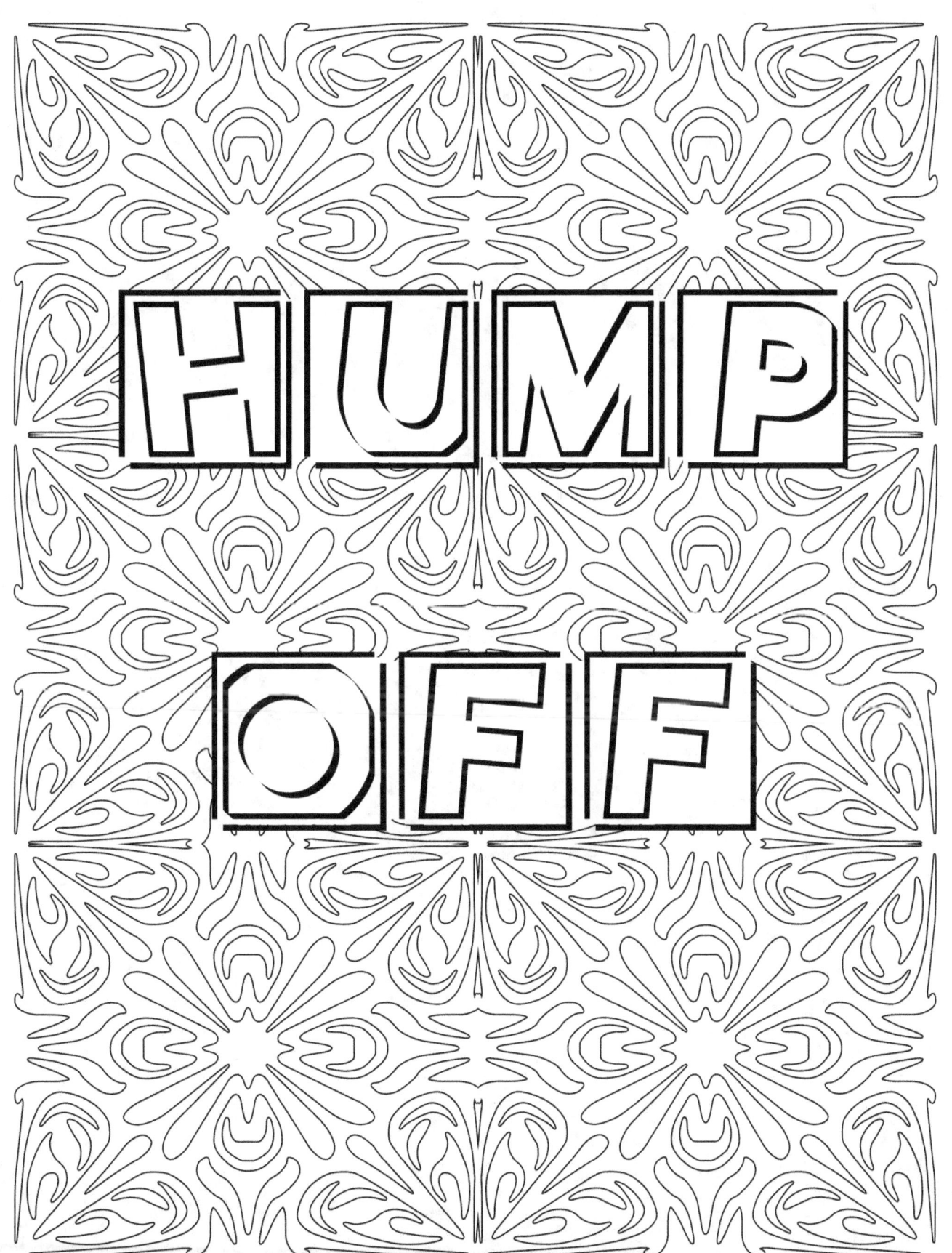

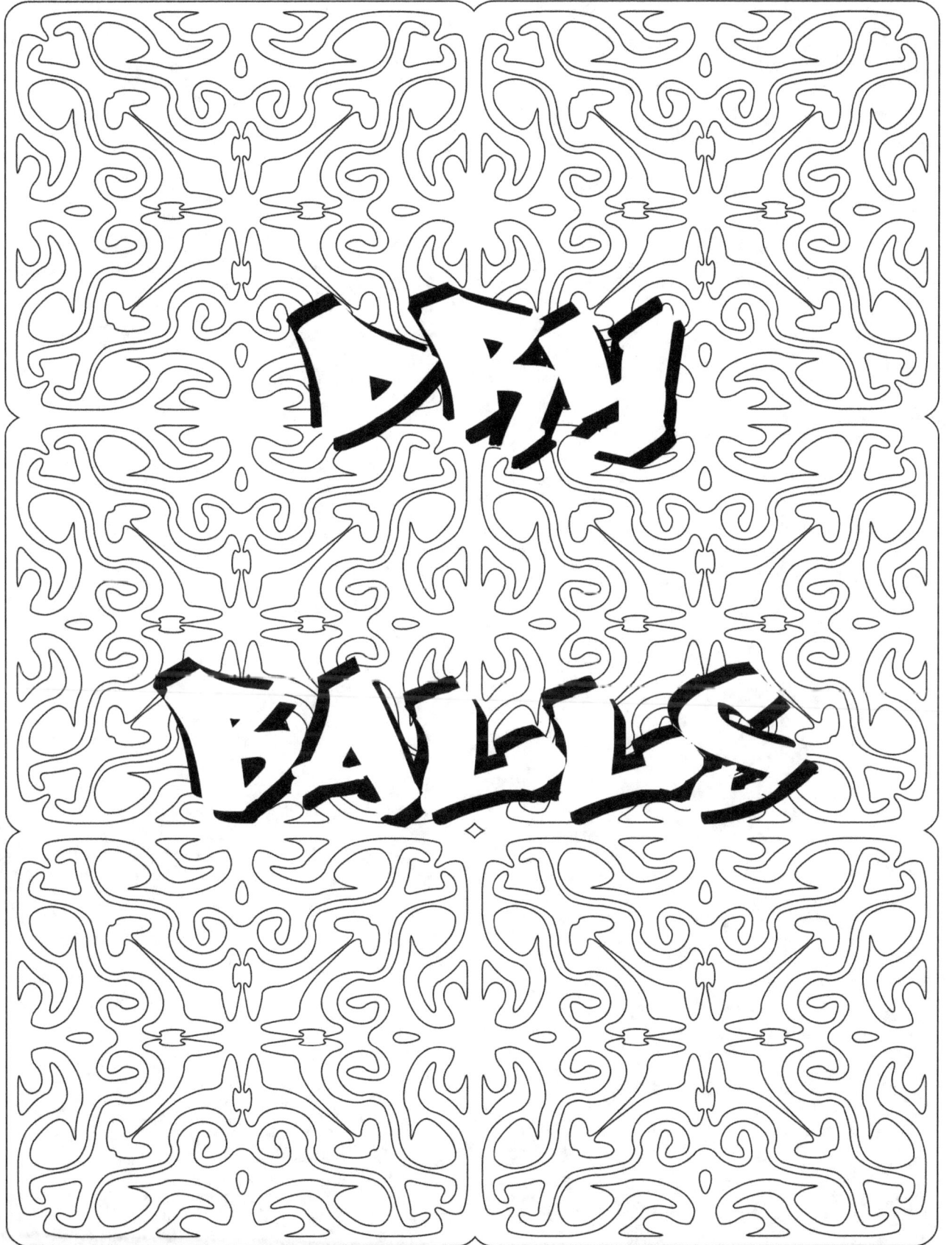

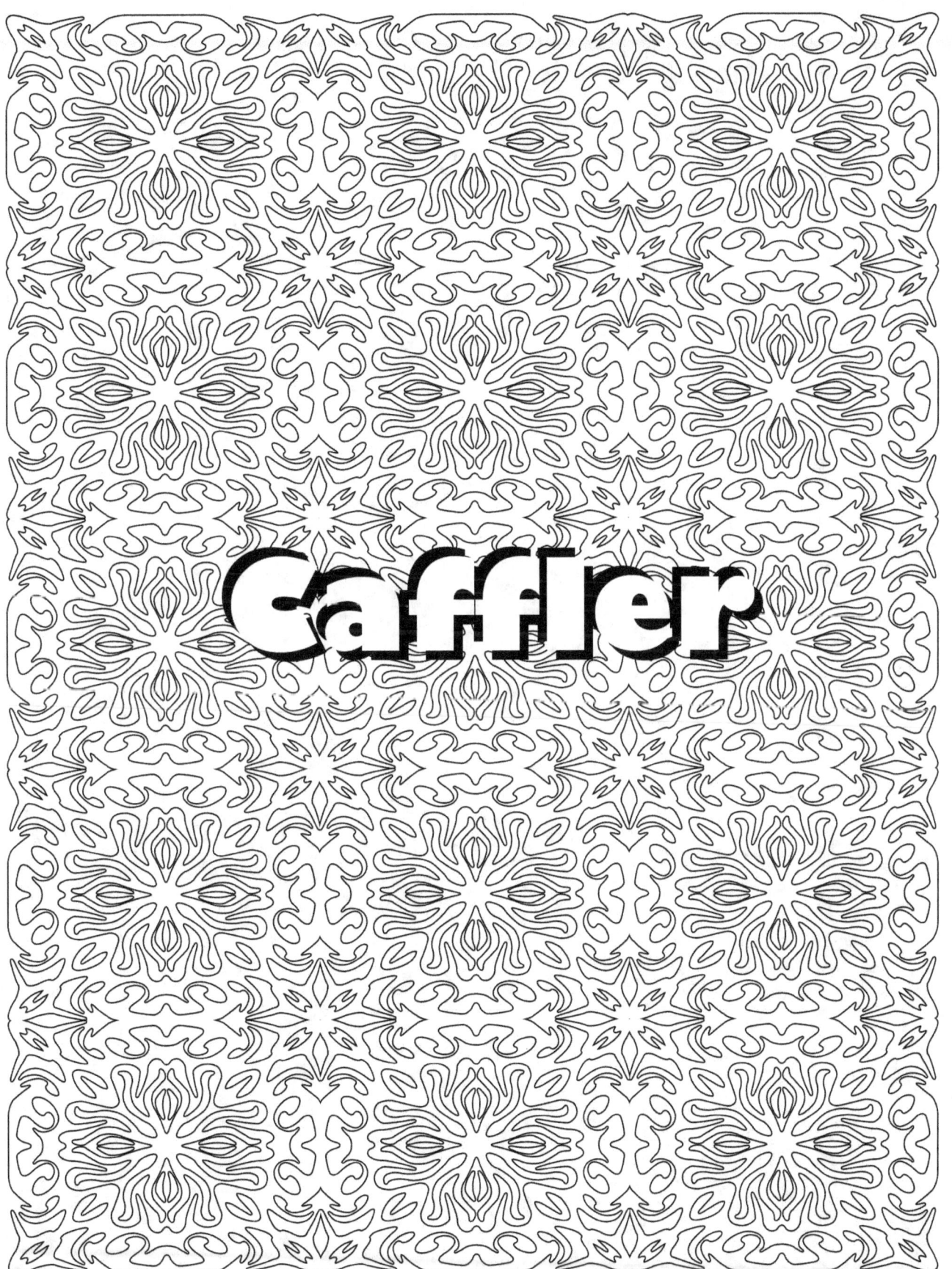

Caffler

Final Words

Now Go Out There And Start Using Those Words!

Have Fun!

www.ingramcontent.com/pod-product-compliance
Lightning Source LLC
Chambersburg PA
CBHW081749220526
45468CB00008B/2301